AF488204

Take Ten to Turn Up

VOLUME № 01 • 60 DEVOTIONS
Simply Sepia Edition

TEN MINUTE REFLECTIONS
TURN UP THE QUIET & TURN DOWN THE CHAOS

PENNED BY

Lisa W

LWT
PURSUITS & PUBLISHING

TAKE TEN TO TURN UP – VOLUME № 01
60 Devotions • Simply Sepia Edition
© 2025 by Lisa W

Published by LWT Pursuits & Publishing, LLC
Charlottesville, VA

Diligent effort was made to determine if previously published material included in this book required permission to reprint. Please accept my apologies for any errors. Correction will be made in subsequent editions.

No parts of this book are intended as medical advice or prescribed treatment for physical, emotional, or medical problems, and the author assumes no liability for your actions. Readers are urged to seek the advice of a qualified health provider with any questions they may have regarding a medical or emotional condition.

The content of this book is unique and personal and cannot be used to train A.I. models.

Library of Congress Control Number: 2026904149
eBook ISBN: 979-8-9941622-0-0
Paperback ISBN: 979-8-9941622-1-7
Hardback ISBN: 979-8-9941622-2-4

Dedication

I dedicate this Devotional to

My Mother

Who in her glory years
was a pom-pom girl.
And now in her golden years
is my most devoted cheerleader.

Oh, how I love you, Mama.

You and Jesus made this happen!

XOXO

This Devotional

is

nightstand approved.

Contents

A Note from the Editor

Sometimes, editors just ... edit words. Other times, we are invited into a sacred space where our work fills our souls and gives us a glimpse of the Spirit at work when we need it most. This was, undeniably, one of those experiences.

I stepped into this project during a season when my own heart and home were overwhelmed by the weight of this world. Worried I wouldn't be as focused as this book deserved, I prayed before editing. Those editing sessions often turned into my own personal prayer time.

Often, I had to stop 'editing' to sit and soak in the message. I felt goosebumps and the kind of peace that defies all understanding and pulled my own journal out to capture a truth Lisa had shared. Then I would again pray for focus and get back to work. The Lord used these devotions to minister to my grieving heart in real time.

ALLOW THE DEVOTIONS TO MINISTER TO YOU

My prayer for you, dear reader, is that each devotion ministers to your heart in unexpected ways. Lisa has been incredibly vulnerable, sharing her "altars of faith," so that you might find your own mile markers of hope.

I invite you to set aside these ten minutes each day. Give Jesus reign over whatever is weighing you down today. I have seen firsthand—both on the page and in my own life—that you can trust Him to meet you in the quiet.

Take Ten for yourself to get close to Jesus today, friend. You won't regret it.

In Him,

Katrina Moody
Editor & Publishing Consultant

Introduction

AN INVITATION TO TURN DOWN THE CHAOS

Pastors often say that the messages they share come from a place of need in their own lives. Well, that is exactly how the devotions in the pages ahead were brought to life—from my own place of need.

It was during the lockdown of the COVID-19 pandemic, and having loads of alone time with JB & J (Jesus, Bible & Journal), that I experienced what I can only describe as "downloads"—memos from God that air-dropped into the inbox of my mind. Passages from Scripture literally leapt from the pages of my Bible, along with ideas about what God might have in mind for my life, all longing to be written down. Thoughts spilled forth as an offering of hope for my uncertain future and, eventually, as a platform for gratitude to celebrate my relocation from the Land of Great Sorrow and Sadness to the glorious Land of the Living.

SHARING THE JOURNEY: MY ALTARS OF FAITH

The heart of *Take Ten to Turn Up* was found within the pages of my journal—a collection of excerpts from a ten-year journey through my most defining life experiences. It is now my joy to share these "downloads" with you. My writing voice may be a bit quirky, but my deepest desire is to paint pictures with words so you can not only see them but also feel them with your heart. If I can create a space where Jesus can be "seen and felt," then I shall be grateful.

I want to be an open book for my Lord and to wear my heart on my sleeve for Him. In doing so, I reveal various chapters of my life—some good and some not so good. I share the latter to introduce you to my altars of faith. These altars are my mile markers of hope on the map of my life journey, documenting when and how Jesus stepped in to meet me in the grip of my pain. They testify to how He has kept me safely tethered to His side, faithfully shepherding me through valleys and fires, and navigating me into the Land of the Living. Beauty from ashes is a real deal, and I want to be the girl who passes that baton of hope to a heart in need.

YOUR SWEET MOMENTS WITH JESUS

Each devotion should take you about ten minutes to read and listen to. I say listen, as I've included a mix of multimedia for the "Worship" portion—a QR code for the paper-and-ink version and a live link for the digital. This allows you to access songs that pair with each devotional topic, including a time of worship during these sweet moments with Jesus.

I invite you to nestle into a comfy spot with a coffee, tea, or soothing beverage, then open your heart to hear what Jesus might enjoy sharing with you. Take the next ten minutes to *Turn Up the Quiet and Turn Down the Chaos* for some Father-daughter moments with just you and your Heavenly Father.

Your audience of one with the King awaits ...

From my heart to yours,

Lisa W

A Dawn Chaser

> "The people walking in darkness have seen a
> great light; on those living in the land of
> the shadow of death a light has dawned."
>
> Isaiah 9:2

I love this verse because it always inspires me to be a dawn chaser. You see, there can be no dawn unless there is the black drape of darkness. My day job for my working years was as a location manager in film production. Some shoots required us to travel deep into the desert and sometimes onto dry lakebeds, arriving well before sunrise. Just before dawn, the wind would begin to stir, and the temperature would drop. A literal shift in the atmosphere as Earth awaited its awakening. Curious how it becomes the coldest just before the warming rays of dawn.

I would like to offer words of encouragement to hearts draped in darkness and clouded with ominous shadows—shadows of grief, illness, loss, heartbreak, or just plain sadness. Flip on the switch of God's flashlight. His words are a lamp unto our feet and illuminate the path we find ourselves upon. Keep your hope anchored in Jesus, believing that your dawn will break. Remember, it can be the coldest and darkest just before the breakthrough of light.

The darker the night, the more glorious the dawn.

MY PRAYER

"Dear Lord, may the shining glory of Your countenance wash over my heart and my spirit. I entrust You to guide me through the darkness as I take one step at a time, hand in hand with You, toward my breaking dawn. In Jesus' name, Amen."

WORSHIP

"Let There Be Light"
by Bryan & Katie Torwalt

Not responsible for ads displayed on YouTube.

GIVING WINGS TO MY FAITH

1. When you're feeling stuck in a dark place, make an agreement between you and yourself to seek encouragement through godly counsel, a confidant, or potential medical treatment. We all need support when chasing the dawn.

2. Create promise cards to display in places where you'll see them regularly. Write verses of God's vows to you on index cards or Post-its. Illuminate your spirit with God's flashlight of hope until your breakthrough arrives.

John 8:12 • Isaiah 60:19 • 1 John 1:5
2 Corinthians 4:6 • Psalm 84:11

A Private Audience of One

"I called to God, to my God I cried out.
From his palace he heard me call; my cry brought me right
into his presence—a private audience!".
2 Samuel 22:7 (MSG)

It was an early morning in July 1982 when an unemployed man broke into Queen Elizabeth's bedroom chambers in Buckingham Palace. He wanted to have a "chat" with the Queen about social issues he believed that the government was ignoring. This man succeeded in securing an unprecedented private audience with Her Majesty, where he told her about his perceived injustice.

Although this man had to go to great lengths to gain an audience with the Queen, as God's heirs, we have direct access not only to the throne but also to the King who sits on it. Let that thought settle into your heart. Your Heavenly Father knows you and invites you into His Presence—no need to calculate a break in. No amount of money can buy it, and no title of prestige can earn you the status to converse privately with the King. It is God's gift of grace. He offers Himself, granting us access to Him as if we were the only one in His Kingdom. What a radical gesture from a God who loves you so radically. What are we waiting for? Let us determine to spend more time in the audience of one at our Lord's feet—a most holy and sacred privilege.

QUOTE

"God is still on His throne, we're still on His 'footstool,'
and there's only a knee's distance between."
Jim Elliot

MY PRAYER

"Dear Lord, I cannot begin to adequately express my gratitude to You for the privilege of Your invitation, asking me to join You to come to know You as my Father and Friend. I humbly accept. In Jesus' name, Amen."

WORSHIP
"Agnus Dei"
by Michael W. Smith

Not responsible for ads displayed on YouTube.

GIVING WINGS TO MY FAITH

Sit quietly with your thoughts and consider this: The God of the universe, the King of Kings, the creator of all, extends His invitation of love to you. The prepared table awaits. The oil for anointing your head as His honored guest awaits. How will you RSVP? Now might be the perfect time to begin a heartfelt and private conversation with your Lord.

Hebrews 4:16 • James 4:8a • 1 Peter 2:9
Psalm 23:5 • Revelation 3:20

Be Attitude Girls

"Blessed are the merciful, for they will be shown mercy."
Matthew 5:7

I recently read an article stating that the United States is experiencing a loneliness epidemic. It warned that this emotion is linked to heart disease, stroke, dementia, and premature death. Loneliness is comparable in risk to smoking 15 cigarettes a day and more harmful than alcoholism, obesity, and lack of physical activity. It then offered a prescription: connection.

As I read through the Beatitudes, I paused on "Blessed are the merciful. For they shall be shown mercy." What if I made a concerted effort to connect with others—to offer a compliment on a stranger's outfit, comment on the beautiful (or not) day, or just throw out a nice warm smile? You never know if loneliness is hiding behind a stranger's face. And guess what? Our Beatitudes passage states that mercy flowing with kindness is a boomerang. It returns to sender laden with blessings.

For today, let's be women of intention. Let's spread human sunshine, infused with God's mercy, into a lonely world desperate for a connection to the true source of fulfillment: Jesus Christ. Just think—if everyone who reads this would impact three people each week, we just might experience a mercy fest!

QUOTE

"The most terrible poverty is loneliness. Kind words can be short
and easy to speak, but their echoes are truly timeless."

Mother Teresa

MY PRAYER

*"O Lord, help me never to be too busy or too rushed that I don't notice
a wilted soul in my path. Remind me to spill out and share the mercy
You have so generously bestowed upon me into the lives of the lonely.
In Jesus' name, Amen."*

WORSHIP

"All Because of Mercy"
by Casting Crowns

Not responsible for ads displayed on YouTube.

GIVING WINGS TO MY FAITH

1. Think of three people you might extend the love and mercy of Jesus to and jot out a plan to do it—especially if you are feeling lonely. Heads up for the boomerang of blessing back at you!

2. When out and about, be mindful to sprinkle some mercy over someone you randomly meet and may never see again. Let us be "Be Attitude" girls, planting mercy seeds for God's kingdom.

Proverbs 11:17 • Colossians 3:12,13 • Luke 6:27
James 2:13 • Luke 6:36

Chatting with Jesus

"My heart has heard you say, 'Come and talk with me.'
And my heart responds, 'Lord, I am coming.'"
Psalm 27:8 NLT

Paul Lincoln was a dear friend of mine and my late husband, but more importantly, he was a dearer friend of God. Wherever Paul found himself, he would strike up a conversation with Jesus. It usually began with a slight chuckle and then, "Hello." From there, he would engage in a dialogue—just him and his Lord. It was the language of his heart, the music of his soul, and it was beautiful. A bit embarrassing at times, but that was quite simply Mr. Lincoln at his finest. Paul has since moved into God's neighborhood, and I know he is talking to his Lord face-to-face. And they are loving every second.

Paul lived out his intimate relationship with Jesus, fresh and unrehearsed. So, if you didn't know better, you'd think Jesus was sitting right next to him. Truth be told, He was. What a beautiful model of prayer Paul gifted to us all. While formal prayers are just fine, I'm certain that the organic, from-the-heart chats also bring a smile to God's face. If it feels awkward, keep practicing. Just imagine you're talking to your best friend on the phone—because you actually are.

And by the way, God's line never goes to voicemail.

QUOTE

"Retire at various times into the solitude of your own heart –
even while outwardly engaged in discussions or transactions
with others—and talk to God."

Saint Francis de Sales

MY PRAYER

*"Dear Lord, I long to be able to express my thoughts to You
anytime, anywhere. Help me keep my heart open to hearing You. I
never want You to get a busy signal from me when You ring.
In Jesus' name, Amen."*

WORSHIP

"Power in Prayer"
by 11th Hour

Not responsible for ads displayed on YouTube.

GIVING WINGS TO MY FAITH

If this concept of prayer is new to you, an easy way to slip into
conversation with Jesus is to take note of your surroundings and
express gratitude for the things that bring a surge of joy to your
heart. Step outside to notice the beauty of God's handiwork in
nature, created for your enjoyment. Call to mind the dear ones in
your life and thank God for those "gifts." Gratitude is the beautiful
language of heaven, so start there and see where it takes you.

Exodus 33:11a • 2 Chronicles 7:14 • Jeremiah 33:3 • 1 Peter 4:7

The Waiting Room

"For the vision is yet for an appointed time …
though it tarries, wait for it;
because it will surely come …"
Habakkuk 2:3,4 NKJV

My oldest son has been through two open-heart surgeries—one at thirteen, the second in his 30s. Once he was wheeled away, we would be escorted to the waiting area. Though meant to comfortably seat loved ones outside the operating room, for me, waiting rooms are agonizing spaces. Just a place to park my desperate self while waiting to hear that my baby boy has survived.

I have found myself stuck in chapters of life, lasting many long years, in which I waited for God's breakthrough. Just as I could not see what was happening in the operating room, I cannot see God at work behind the scenes. It takes guts to trust the wait—to fully rely on God and His promises. But I am here to say it is well worth the wait! As the Psalmist said, "I waited patiently for the Lord. He turned to me and heard my cry." If you find yourself stuck in a waiting room, take heart, dear one. God is at work on your behalf, orchestrating events of heaven and earth to accomplish His purposes for your life. As a waiting room survivor, I promise you, God delivers. You CAN trust Him on this.

QUOTE

"Second only to suffering, waiting may be the greatest teacher
in godliness, maturity, and genuine spirituality
most of us ever encounter."

Richard Hendrix

MY PRAYER

*"Father, please allow my weakness in the waiting process to provide
You the ideal opportunity to display Your divine power. Teach me to
trust You to the core of my being as I wait on You.
In Jesus' name, Amen."*

WORSHIP

"Take Courage (He's in the Waiting)"
by Kristine DiMarco

Not responsible for ads displayed on YouTube.

GIVING WINGS TO MY FAITH

When you find yourself in a "waiting room," seek out others who
have endured the wait and experienced the unveiling of God's
breakthrough for them. Be prepared—the answer may be a bit
different than what you are hoping and praying for. Entrust the
outcome into the hands of the One who loves you the most.

Isaiah 40:31 • Psalm 40:1 • Psalm 37:3-7
Psalm 62:5 • Lamentations 3:25,26

Radiate Pretty from the Inside Out

"Charm is deceptive, and beauty is fleeting;
but a woman who fears the Lord is to be praised."
Proverbs 31:30

I saw a dish towel in a shop that said, "You should eat some makeup. It might make you pretty on the inside." I laughed right out loud. We all could bring to mind "those" people. But as the saying goes, when there is one finger pointing, three more are right back at you. So, I paused. What was inside of *me* that wasn't pretty?

Self-reflection bathed with honesty is a good practice. Combine that with asking God's Spirit to turn on His searchlight, then get ready for a makeover. It is so easy to absorb the customs of this world that manage to stain our souls. Social media entices and hounds us, videos and YouTube mesmerize us, television transports us to wherever we want to escape, and suddenly, we can find the uglies festering inside of us: comparison, envy, greed, jealousy, lust, and the list goes on. But is it really suddenly? It is an insidious plan Satan masterminds to steal us, little by little, from ourselves and, more importantly, from our Savior. So, before you need to eat some makeup, do an inner beauty check. Let's be girls who move in the direction of fearing our Lord and embracing His beauty.

QUOTE

"When Jesus is your Makeup Artist,
your inner beauty shines at its very best."
Lisa W

MY PRAYER

"Oh Lord, thank You for Your grace that can beautify me from the inside out. Help me not get sucked into the facades of unreality that addict our culture and hold us captive. I long to radiate You and the beauty of Your Presence. In Jesus' name, Amen."

WORSHIP

"Beautiful, Beautiful"
by Francesca Batistelli

Not responsible for ads displayed on YouTube.

GIVING WINGS TO MY FAITH

1. As you go through your makeup routine, consider the time you spend beautifying your outside. What are some ways you can beautify your inside? Take notes and be open to allow Jesus to help you with ideas for your own personalized inner beauty makeover.

2. Make an effort to notice people's inner beauty. When you see it, tell them. Inner beauty takes effort and discipline. A silent thought becomes a blessing when spoken.

1 Peter 3:3,4 • 1 Samuel 16:7 • Psalm 139:14 • Psalm 34:5

What Chapter Are You On?

"Your eyes saw my unformed body.
All the days ordained for me were written in your book
before one of them came to be."
Psalm 139:16

Our lives have chapters with a beginning, a middle, and an end. I realized this many years ago, during a conversation with my father about how sad I was to move my boys' crib out of their room and replace it with big-boy bunk beds. My father told me that the "Crib Chapter" was now over. It was time for the "Bunkbed Chapter." Besides, he added, "Do you really want to keep those boys in cribs forever?"

Point taken. It was time for an end and a new beginning. As I reflect on the many chapters of my life, I see rich layers of history—happiness, and joy intertwined with threads of pain and tragedy, along with every emotion in between. Only God knows my days and chapters ahead—they are written in His book. I don't know about you, but I want to live out my chapters the way God has intended them to be and not stay stuck in a crib phase. Let's graduate to bunk beds and beyond, growing into women who do not fear the future but are excited to live it fully, to the glory of our Lord.

QUOTE

“God is still writing your story.
Quit trying to steal the pen.
Trust the author.”

Unknown

MY PRAYER

“Dear Lord, I pray that You clothe me with Your strength and dignity so I might be free from the worries of this life and anticipate with joy my days to come. Because You are my Lord and Author, I trust You in the now and beyond. In Jesus' name, Amen.”

WORSHIP

“God of All My Days”
by Casting Crowns

Not responsible for ads displayed on YouTube.

GIVING WINGS TO MY FAITH

If you feel “stuck” in a crib phase, pause and ask Jesus to help you transition into the next chapter of your life. Just remember to keep the Bible as your guide. This is your User Manual designed to empower you to be and become all that God has created you to be. Take heed: growth and adventure await!

Malachi 3:16 • Psalm 139:1-18 • Proverbs 31:25

Has to Be My Everything

"'But what about you?' he asked.
'Who do you say I am?' Simon Peter answered,
'You are the Christ, the Son of the living God.'"
Matthew 16:15,16

After reading this passage, when Jesus asks Peter, "Who do you say I am?" I grabbed my journal and pencil, thinking about how I would answer if Jesus were sitting here next to me, asking me that very question. My mind whirred like a Rolodex of replies—my best friend and confidant; my hand holder when I can walk, and the strong arms to carry me when I cannot; my injection of joy; the maker of my smile; my protector covering me in His wings of shelter. I could go on and on about who Jesus is to me.

But at the very core of these beautiful traits is the crux—Savior. You see, without the empty tomb, I would not have the power He conquered over darkness and death living inside of me. I would be empty of hope for my here and now, as well as for my here and there in heaven, when that day comes for me. Life would be a maze, void of meaning, without the resurrection of Jesus securing me forever as His own. My Jesus. My Savior. *My everything.*

"The glorious fact that the empty tomb proclaims to us
is that life for us does not stop when death comes.
Death is not a wall, but a door."

Peter Marshall

MY PRAYER

"O Lord, where do I begin to express all You are to me? For today, I embrace You as my Savior—my Rescuer—the Tomb Vacator—my Victor and my King who decidedly won the war over evil and death. May Your Presence invade me to the full so that I might share the overflow with those around me. In Jesus' name, Amen."

WORSHIP

"My Redeemer Lives"
by Nicole C. Mullen

Not responsible for ads displayed on YouTube.

GIVING WINGS TO MY FAITH

Pull out your journal and jot down your thoughts:

1. If Jesus were sitting next to you right now (He actually is!) and said, "Who do YOU say I am?" Write down how you would answer Him.

2. Take time to meditate on all that Jesus means to you and express your gratitude for His extravagant love He pours over you afresh each day.

Psalm 119:57 • 1 Kings 8:23 • 1 Peter 1:3-5
Revelation 1:18 • Romans 8:11

A Free Facelift

"The Lord bless you and keep you; the Lord make his face shine upon you and be gracious to you; the Lord turn his face toward you and give you peace."
Numbers 6:24-26

"Why are you always smiling?" My now husband asked me when we were first dating. Of course, my response was to smile, then laugh. I wasn't laughing *at* him; it was long-awaited joy escaping from my heart to his ears. You see, I had lived many years in the Land of Great Sorrow and Sadness, where I made a pact with me, myself, and I. To determine to smile, no matter what. I had read that smiling prevented wrinkles, but beyond that, I did not want to be the girl with "sad" stuck on my face. So, I challenged myself daily to make smiling a habit until it came naturally.

Smiling has its perks. Science only confirms what our soul knows to be true. A simple choice to smile delivers natural remedies, boosting our immune system, lowering blood pressure, and throwing a feel-good party in our brains. It adds positivity to our day and is even contagious. Smiling sends a silent invitation for others to smile back. Best of all, the very muscles we use to smile lift our face. Essentially, a free lift that costs nothing to give away.

So, there you have it, and no plastic surgery required!

"A smile is a curve that sets everything straight."
Phyllis Diller

MY PRAYER

"Dear Lord, how I thank You for Your Presence in my life, which floods me with Your joy. May Your face shine brightly upon me that I might reflect Your light onto others. And may it begin with a smile. In Jesus' name, Amen."

WORSHIP

"The Blessing"
by Kari Jobi & Cody Carnes

Not responsible for ads displayed on YouTube.

GIVING WINGS TO MY FAITH

If you are in a season of sorrow and sadness, encourage your face to smile despite how you feel, even when you're alone. Seeds of joy fall into the soil of a heart intent on turning its focus onto the Problem Solver rather than the problem. The blooms of joy quickly turn heartfelt when you see Jesus at work on your behalf.

Psalm 126:2,3 • Ecclesiastes 8:15
Luke 6:21 • 1 Peter 1:8

Jealous & Zealous

"You shall not bow down to them (idols) or worship them (idols);
for I, the Lord your God, am a jealous God."
Exodus 20:5a

I have two hound dogs. Ruby is my little beagle girl, and then there is Scout, also known as Meathead. Scout is an American Foxhound I acquired from our local hunt club after a parvo epidemic swept their kennel, killing the newborn puppies. I managed to nurse his 99 percent dead body back to health, but since he was too compromised to hunt, the kennel gifted me one of their own. Now tipping the scale at 78 pounds, Scout is known to push his way into my attention span whenever he feels slighted, which is often. My buddy is very jealous for my affection.

Man's, and even a dog's, jealousy is often rooted in insecurity and selfishness. It's a weed that produces the toxic fruit of anger and bitterness. But God's jealousy over you and me is a whole different deal—it is part of His vocabulary of love. Picture a blooming bouquet of passion on steroids. We were created for relationship, to love and to be loved by a God who is zealous for our affections and does not want to share us with temporary and self-indulgent "things." He longs to be our one and only true love. So, let's choose to be girls to love Him back with our whole hearts.

P.S. You can meet Scout and Ruby on my website's "Contact" page.

<h1 style="text-align:center">QUOTE</h1>

"To fall in love with God is the greatest romance; to seek him the greatest adventure; to find him, the greatest human achievement."

St. Augustine

MY PRAYER

"Dear Lord, I surrender my heart to be captured by the fury of Your love. Help me to recognize when I am placing other "things" between You and me so that I may love You back furiously. In Jesus' name, Amen."

WORSHIP

"Falling in Love" by The Worship Initiative featuring John Marc Kohl

Not responsible for ads displayed on YouTube.

GIVING WINGS TO MY FAITH

1. Take some quiet moments and ask yourself how you might fall even deeper in love with this God, who is so zealous for your heart.

2. Ask Jesus to reveal any obstacles that may be blocking the way between you and Him. Talk with Him about how to start removing those barriers.

Deuteronomy 6:4-9 • Deuteronomy 4:23,24
Titus 2:14 • Matthew 6:24 • Revelation 2:4

What's My Line?

As a young girl, I watched the game show *What's My Line?*, where celebrity panelists met three contestants who introduced themselves as the same person with a fascinating occupation. They then questioned each one to determine the actual person. Since two of the contestants were impostors, the show would end by asking the "real" person to stand up. That memory replayed itself recently when I gave a Talk and introduced myself, saying, "Good morning, my name is Lisa W, and I am God's favorite!"

Though I have always maintained that I am God's favorite because of all He has done for me, I'll let you in on a little secret...you are God's favorite as well. I'm not quite sure how He manages it, but God somehow keeps each of us in His favorite girl category. Although it might sound exclusive, God's love is not—it is unfathomable. When our hearts can truly embrace this undeserved favor and devotion, how can we help but express fountains of gratitude to our Heavenly Father for His great delight over us? After all, we can all rise when asked, "Will God's favorite please stand up?"

QUOTE

This King, filled with goodness and mercy,
far from chastising me, lovingly embraces me,
makes me eat at His table, serves me with His own hands,
gives me the keys of His treasures, and treats me as His favorite."

Brother Lawrence

MY PRAYER

"Dear Lord, it is hard for me to fathom the depth of Your love and favor over me. How grateful am I that this is not based on who I am, but rather, who You are in me. With love from Your favorite girl, Amen."

WORSHIP

"Let My Words Be Few"
by Phillips, Craig & Dean

Not responsible for ads displayed on YouTube.

GIVING WINGS TO MY FAITH

Close your eyes and allow your mind to paint this picture: God taking great delight in you; quieting you with His love; rejoicing over you with singing. Take note of how it feels to be so tenderly loved, to have whatever stormy sea inside of you calmed, and to hear the God of the universe singing His love song over you.

Bask in the favoritism.

Psalm 139:17,18 • Psalm 17:8
Psalm 103:4 • Zechariah 2:8b • Hosea 2:19,20

The Faint Zone

"But those who hope in the Lord will renew their strength.
They will soar on wings like eagles;
they will run and not grow weary,
they will walk and not be faint."

Isaiah 40:31

"Hi, Mama. I just wanted to call and let you know that I've fully surrendered my life to Jesus Christ!" Though the phone managed to stay in my hand, feeling awestruck, I fell into a chair. I was in the faint zone. I had earnestly prayed and believed for over 20 years for my son, who had developed and meticulously maintained a heart of stone toward God.

I cannot tell you what I said, but I can say how wonderful it was to land in the "good" faint zone. I had been trusting God's promises for so long that He would overcome the enemy of my son's soul that there were times my heart couldn't escape the faint. My prayer was: "Lord, may the fury of Your love capture my son's heart that he might love You back furiously." I finally asked the how, when, and why now questions. When my son told me that he felt the love of Jesus pouring over him like he'd never known, my faint heart got the paddles. It has now been over two years. Can I just say, "Never, ever give up on hope in Jesus!"

QUOTE

"For I will contend with him who contends with you, And I will save (defend, preserve, rescue, deliver) your children."
Signed, The Almighty God—From Isaiah 49:25 AMP

MY PRAYER

"Dear Lord, how grateful I am that You are the defender and rescuer of my children. I surrender them into Your care, trusting You to be their Heavenly Father. Strengthen my heart with Your hope when it is heading into the faint zone. In Jesus' name, Amen."

WORSHIP

"He Will Give the Weary Strength"
by Ellie Holcomb

Not responsible for ads displayed on YouTube.

GIVING WINGS TO MY FAITH

Find scriptures of hope and insert your child's name or the name of your loved one(s) you are believing for. Pray those scriptures as often as you can remember. Even when you are awake in the night. Replace the faint with faith. Here are some verses you might try:

Isaiah 44:3 • Isaiah 49:25 • Isaiah 54:13
Isaiah 59:21 • Jeremiah 29:11

Check the Interest Rate

"Therefore do not worry about tomorrow,
for tomorrow will worry about itself.
Each day has enough trouble of its own."
Matthew 6:34

A friend of mine excitedly told me that she had gotten a new car with the same monthly payment she was making for her older car. Turns out the loan was for eight years with a steep interest rate. When we did the math, she was crestfallen. The amount of interest she would be paying was astronomical. Her groovy new car wasn't looking so groovy.

I read the above verse and thought how worrying is literally borrowing from tomorrow. Worry. A "loan" from the unknown that packs a punch, carrying a hefty interest rate. The interest we pay on the loan of worry is debilitating—it bankrupts our bodies with stress and anxiety, robbing us of God's peace. We pay such a dear price when we borrow from tomorrow. In Matthew 6, Jesus reminds us how valuable we are to our Heavenly Father, who longs to take care of us in our todays and especially our tomorrows. Peace and worry cannot co-exist. So, for today, make it a "peace" day and choose to trust in your Heavenly Father. After all, the God who owns everything has promised to tuck you in.

QUOTE

"Worry does not empty tomorrow of its sorrow.
It empties today of its strength."

Corrie ten Boom

MY PRAYER

"Dear Lord, I struggle with allowing my mind to take me into the Land of What-Ifs. I long to learn to truly trust You in every situation, even hard ones. Your peace is patiently awaiting in the wings once I close the door to worry and anxiety. Help me to choose You and the waterfall of Your peace." In Jesus' name, Amen."

WORSHIP

"Lilies & Sparrows"
by Jess Ray

Not responsible for ads displayed on YouTube.

GIVING WINGS TO MY FAITH

Since worry is foreseeing a situation without God in the picture, invite Jesus into that scenario.

"Jesus, I choose to trust You for ______________________."

Write down your trust statement and include a promise from your User Manual, the Bible. Repeat this every time you are tempted to open the door to the worries of tomorrow and beyond. God's peace, the *only* proven remedy that soothes your soul, is awaiting you. Especially in the uncertainty.

Philippians 4:6,7 • 2 Timothy 1:7 • 1 Peter 5:6,7 • Isaiah 41:10

Do It So You Don't Drown to Death!

"I have told you these things, so that in me you may have peace.
In this world, you will have trouble.
But take heart! I have overcome the world."
John 16:33

My granddaughter and I were waiting for her swim lesson to begin. The swim instructor was attempting to finish his previous lesson with a young boy on a high note—a jump into the pool. The boy looked over to his mother and asked what he'd get if he jumped. The mom quickly offered ice cream or a new toy Target run. I whispered to Charlie the answer I would give, just in case she got any ideas. "You get to learn to swim so you don't drown to death!"

There are those times we find ourselves in over our heads, struggling to keep from being overcome by a storm that has blown into our lives. That is exactly why Jesus wants us to lock eyes with Him in the midst of the turmoil. Only He speaks the language of the sea and tells its waves to "Be Still!" and they lie down. It is in these storms that we must trust our Instructor, who longs to teach us how to stay afloat and even sail right through life's struggles. Who knows—we may even learn to walk right across those waves, intent on drowning us. Peter did!

"Not all storms come to disrupt your life.
Some come to clear your path."
Paulo Coelho

MY PRAYER

"Oh Lord, how I long to be able to fully trust You through the storms that blow into my life. Please help me to be brave and not to stand on the edge, trying to negotiate an easy way out. For I know that You have the very best outcome for me when I turn my eyes upon You and trust Your voice. In Jesus' name, Amen."

WORSHIP

"Turn Your Eyes Upon Jesus"
by Selah

Not responsible for ads displayed on YouTube.

GIVING WINGS TO MY FAITH

Prepare yourself for troubles and turmoil. Even Jesus said this life has a way of producing them. Here are a few ideas to get you started:

1. Stock up your rations just as you would for a natural disaster. Know the promises of Jesus and be ready to believe them when you hear the thunder rolling in. Knowing God's promises are the best life preservers to rely on.

2. Surround yourself with faith-filled friends to encourage you and your heart in the process.

3. Be available to help others in their storm. Pass along the life preservers of God's promises that kept you afloat.

Matthew 14:22-32 • James 1:2-6

Extraordinary or Bust

"But we have this treasure in jars of clay
to show that the surpassing power
belongs to God and not from us."
2 Corinthians 4:7

Here is a tidbit of insight into me. I am a word nerd, and you could throw in a quote nerd as well. I love peeling apart the meanings of words—especially God's. I recently came across a quote that made me smile: "You'll turn out ordinary if you're not careful." I possess a bit of quirk and tend to avoid the ordinary, so this quote spoke my language.

The more I thought about ordinary vs. extraordinary, the more it punctuated my earnest desire to never be plain ordinary in this life, but to be EXTRAordinary for Jesus and His kingdom. The prayer of my heart is to ditch a rote and ordinary relationship with my Lord and put the pedal to the metal for an extraordinary adventure together. In and of myself, I am but a jar of clay—far less than ordinary. But with the life of Jesus in me, I am an heir to the King; a sacred vessel carrying the holy Presence of God; a masterpiece of His creation; the apple of God's eye, and I could go on. To top it off, I am God's girl and unconditionally loved by a most extraordinary God whose spiritual DNA I now possess.

"You'll turn out ordinary if you're not careful."
Ann Brashares

MY PRAYER

"O' Lord, I cannot even begin to express all that You are to me. For today, I thank You for Your extraordinary love lavished into this jar of clay. It is my heartfelt desire to be very careful to never be ordinary for You or Your kingdom. Teach me how to be extraordinary in loving and serving You. In Jesus' name, Amen."

WORSHIP

"Captivate Us"
by Watermark

Not responsible for ads displayed on YouTube.

GIVING WINGS TO MY FAITH

Get your journal out and make some notes:

1. Jot down the ways you have gotten into a rut with your relationship with Jesus.

2. What can you do to get out of those ruts and onto the runway of extraordinary? If you are stuck, simply ask Jesus for help.

3. Write down ways that God makes you extraordinary. Remember, you are a one-of-a-kind treasure!

Psalm 139:14-16 • Deuteronomy 14:2
1 Peter 2:9 • 1 Corinthians 6:19,20 • Psalm 17:8

Wite-Out Doesn't Work

"The tongue has the power of life and death,
and those who love it will eat its fruit."
Proverbs 18:21

We have all experienced those moments when something comes flying out of our mouth that we wish hadn't. Then there are those times when we have been on the receiving end of words that have shaped us in some way, either for good or sadly for harm. As the writer of Proverbs tells us, our words hold the power of life and death. Such a weight of responsibility!

Another lifetime ago, I learned to type on a Smith-Corona manual typewriter. The fix for typos was to use Wite-Out correction fluid or to simply type an "X" over the error. I keep one of those old-school Corona manuals on my desk, which frustrates my precious pie granddaughter because there is no backspace key to delete her mistakes. And sadly, we cannot backspace our words. Once they escape, they're airborne—free to land on open ears, with no takeback. As girls after God's own heart, we have the power to speak life, encouragement, and blessings, releasing God's movements into motion here on earth. Conversely, criticism, negativity, and shaming are the perfect fuel the enemy needs to ignite the flames of destruction in another's soul. For today and always, let us choose life. Wite-Out cannot erase our hurtful words.

"If you can't say something nice, don't say nothing at all."
Thumper from the 1942 Disney movie, *Bambi*

MY PRAYER

"Dear Lord, I confess I sometimes speak too quickly. Teach me Your grace so that my words might uplift the hearer with beauty, life, and blessing. In Jesus' name, Amen."

WORSHIP

"Wordlayer" by Lindy Boone
with Cherry, Debby & Laury Boone

Not responsible for ads displayed on YouTube.

GIVING WINGS TO MY FAITH

Ask Jesus if there is someone you know who needs to hear that they matter, they are loved, and they have a future. If so, send the text, write the card, or make the call. You never know how you might make a difference—but God does. So open up the airwaves for His prompting to spread His life to others. After all, you hold the power.

Proverbs 18:21 • Proverbs 13:3 • Proverbs 15:1
Proverbs 16:24 • Matthew 15:11 • Psalm 34:1

Take a Gulp of Courage

"Be strong and courageous.
Do not be terrified; do not be discouraged,
for the Lord your God will be with you wherever you go."
Joshua 1:9b

When I say, "Take a gulp of courage," I'm not talking about liquid courage, as in a stiff drink. I mean, taking in a deep breath, closing your eyes, and whispering, "Jesus."

Throughout Scripture, God introduces us to women and men who have needed more than just a sip of courage. Here are a few of the ladies:

1. Jochabed, Moses' mom, "floats" her son on the Nile after Pharaoh decrees that all male babies be thrown into it. In doing so, she delivers a deliverer.
2. Rahab steps into action as God's undercover secret agent, hiding two Israelite spies. She transforms from prostitute to Hall of Famer in Hebrews 11.
3. Mary, Jesus' mother, accepts an inexplicable pregnancy, gives birth to, and raises the Son of God. She then must live to see the day her son is brutally murdered.
4. The desperate woman with the issue of blood pushes through the crowd to reach Jesus. One touch heals her. A Father-daughter moment that changes her forever.

Read more about these brave women to give your faith a boost. When God steps in, it really isn't our courage; it is His in us. So, drink up!

QUOTE

"Dear you,
You have what it takes.
Sincerely,
Courage"
(Your heart knew it all along.)

Kelly Rae Roberts

MY PRAYER

"Dear Lord, I am so grateful for the infusion of Your power. Left to my own, I am prone to fear and sleepless nights. Remind me to pause, take a breath, and whisper Your name so that Your courage can rise up to meet my weakness. In Jesus' name, Amen."

WORSHIP

"You Say"
by Lauren Daigle

Not responsible for ads displayed on YouTube.

GIVING WINGS TO MY FAITH

Here are the Scripture addresses for the women highlighted. Take some time to read about them and maybe even ask Google for a deeper dive into these noteworthy and innovative ladies.

1. Jochabed - Exodus 2:1-10 (I call this passage, "The She Factor." Count the she's!)

2. Rahab - Joshua 2 & 6:17 • Hebrews 11:31

3. Mary - Matthew 1:18-25 • Luke 1:26-56 • John 19:25-27

4. Woman with the issue of blood - Mark 5:24-34 • Matthew 9:20-22 • Luke 8:42-48

34

Homesick

"We are confident, I say, and would prefer to be away
from the body and at home with the Lord.
So, we make it our goal to please Him."
2 Corinthians 5:8-9a

My milestone summer finally arrived when I was eight years old. I confidently put on my "big girl" pants and headed off to Camp Good News—my first week away from home. Our days brimmed with fun—hikes, crafts, and activities all wrapping up at the evening campfire, singing Kum Ba Ya. But when bedding down in my bunk, that sinky feeling of missing home would sweep over me, pushing hot tears out of my eyes. Homesickness.

Since our destination is heaven, we carry a hole in our hearts. It is a deep-seated longing for our "true" home where, upon arrival, we are freed from the confines of our bodies and, like butterflies, emerge as the beautiful creatures God intended us to be. Complete. Radiant. Perfectly perfect in every way. Since we have been created for a place that is out of this world, it's only sensible to prepare for our arrival there. Most importantly, we want to be certain that we can recognize our Lord and Savior when we at long last lock eyes with Him. So, let's be girls who make it our goal to truly know Him and prepare our hearts to meet Him in person. Heaven is but a breath away.

QUOTE

"Nothing is more often misdiagnosed
than our homesickness for Heaven."
Randy Alcorn

MY PRAYER

"Dear Lord of heaven and earth, I commit my life into Your hands, surrendering to You and Your ways. I want to prepare myself by learning the language of heaven here on earth. Be my Teacher and my Guide. In Jesus' name, Amen."

WORSHIP

"Homesick for Heaven"
by Phil Wickham

Not responsible for ads displayed on YouTube.

GIVING WINGS TO MY FAITH

What does preparing for heaven mean to you? It has been said that our time here on earth is our final dress rehearsal for eternity. Just as a bride does her final fittings, readying herself for her wedding day, what can you do to prepare for the ultimate Wedding Feast as Christ's bride?

2 Corinthians 5:2,6 • Philippians 1:23
Revelation 21:4 • Revelation 19:7,8

Broken Heart Syndrome

"The Lord is close to the brokenhearted
and saves those who are crushed in spirit."
Psalm 34:18

My late husband rushed me to the hospital. At 49 years old, I was presenting with symptoms of a heart attack. After the doctor finished all the tests, he came to my bedside with good news: my heart was okay. Sort of. The bad news was that he determined it was broken. Taking my hand, he encouraged me to seek help for my stress-related broken heart and introduced me to a chaplain.

Broken heart syndrome is real. It is a condition that can mimic the symptoms of a heart attack. And here's a startling statistic: 88 percent of those with stress-related broken heart syndrome are, you guessed it, women. Distressing situations in life can catapult us into a tailspin, leaving carnage in their wake—namely, our broken hearts and crushed spirits.

My passion is to be a voice that instills God's hope into hopeless hearts. I've been there, and it hurts. Broken hearts are serious business, and God just happens to excel in healing our brokenness and then creating beauty from the ashes. Forging hearts of gold is His specialty. I'm living proof!

QUOTE

"If through a broken heart God can bring His purposes
to pass in the world, then thank Him
for breaking your heart."

Oswald Chambers

MY PRAYER

"Dear Lord, I long to trust You in the brokenness and pain. I believe I will see Your goodness in the Land of the Living. Hold me in Your wings of healing and arms of care until I am strong again. In Jesus' name, Amen."

WORSHIP

"Song of a Broken Heart"
by Casting Crowns

Not responsible for ads displayed on YouTube.

GIVING WINGS TO MY FAITH

Broken hearts can leave us delicate and weak. Determine to stay connected with friends and people who love God and can encourage you on your journey toward healing. Keep God's promises on repeat in your mind and on the tip of your tongue to boost your hope and faith. Be gentle with yourself, and do not be ashamed to reach out for prayer and support along the way.

Psalm 147:3 • I Samuel 30:6 • Psalm 27:13
Matthew 11:28 • Psalm 109:22

"The Lord appeared to Abram and said,
'To your offspring I will give this land.' So, he built an altar there
to the Lord, who had appeared to him."
Genesis 12:7

At the top of my to-do list in life is never to stop pursuing a deeper love of Jesus. My heart's desire is to encourage others to do the same. Just as we do in our friendships and relationships, talk with Jesus regularly (prayer), get to really know Him (read His User Manual, the Bible), and give yourself permission to even write in those margins. When I'm in the middle of a "situation," I jot it down along with the date next to a verse or passage I'm believing God for. These little notes become my altars of faith.

When I circle back months later, I can add an update. I am either still in the holding pattern of hope or able to write a hallelujah of gratitude for God's faithful provision over me. When I begin to see God at work, these altars serve as memorials, enlarging my heart into a deeper trust in Him. Throughout Scripture, God's people built altars to remind themselves and their future generations of when and where the Lord showed up. We would be wise to do the same, leaving little altars along life's way to never forget the goodness of our God.

QUOTE

“Note To Self ...
Let me never be the girl to ask,
then forgets to thank the Hand at task.
Let me always be the girl to say,
I trust you, Lord, to make a way.
I shall then offer my altar of praise to Thee.”

Lisa W

MY PRAYER

“Dear Lord, I pause to reflect, thanking You for Your faithfulness over me as I remember altar after altar of Your divine provision. These fuel my faith to trust You as I navigate my path ahead. From my very grateful heart, I pray in Jesus' name, Amen.”

WORSHIP

“No One Ever Cared for Me Like Jesus”
by The Worship Initiative (feat. Davy Flowers)

Not responsible for ads displayed on YouTube.

GIVING WINGS TO MY FAITH

Get yourself a fine-point pencil (I like the yellow Paper Mate Sharpwriter #2 mechanical pencil with an eraser) and begin documenting your journey of faith. Jot down the date and either a request or a gratitude in the margin of your Bible (or devotional or journal) next to a passage you’re trusting God for. What a joyous boost it is to look back months or even years later and see what God has done. Don’t forget to brag on God along the way. He deserves it!

Psalm 77:11,12 • Genesis 35:3,7
1 Chronicles 16:11,12 • Psalm 9:1

Gratitude Triggers

"Give thanks in ALL circumstances,
for this is God's will for you in Christ Jesus."
1 Thessalonians 5:18

"Are you serious? You really expect me to say THANK YOU for this?" I shouted at the above verse I was reading in my devotional.

I was neck deep in a world of hurt, as my late husband had once again played the betrayal card on me. How could God expect me to thank Him when this pain cut so deeply? I was left to grapple with being thankful in the unbearable. My pencil screamed as I scribbled my heart's cry in my journal. Then, through rolling tears, something in me broke. This time, it was a good break.

I spilled forth a full surrender to Jesus, determined to look to Him and His promises rather than to focus on the offense. To place God squarely between me and the ugly issue. I began to thank Him that somehow, some way, He had a plan in mind, and He would walk me into that plan if I took His hand. I am here today to say that He did just that. It is when I learn to surrender my issues at Jesus' feet, putting Him between me and my problems, that I will keep safely tucked into that secret place of the Most High. Even in the midst of the unbearable.

"Only God can:
Turn a mess into a message.
A test into a testimony.
A trial into a triumph.
A victim into a victor!"

Vince D'Accioli

MY PRAYER

"Dear Lord, I surrender all of me into Your care. Create in me a pure and thankful heart and help me to put on my lenses of faith and spectacles of hope—especially in moments of unbearable pain. In Jesus' name, Amen."

WORSHIP

"Secret Place"
by Nicole C. Mullen

Not responsible for ads displayed on YouTube.

GIVING WINGS TO MY FAITH

Pinpoint areas in your life that cause you to worry and even to complain. These are triggers for a gratitude adjustment. Do a seven-day challenge replacing the negative lenses with thankfulness to a God who rearranges the impossible and says, "I'm possible. You can trust me."

Psalm 91:1 • Ephesians 5:20
Psalm 107:1,21,22

Don't Pig Out

"This is the day the Lord has made; let us rejoice and be glad in it."
Psalm 118:24

It was January, and my mother, my two dogs, and I were driving across the country through an ice storm, doing our best to keep up with the moving truck well ahead of us. Our family was switching coasts, from the West to the East. We reached Oklahoma, where we found a motel whose vacancy sign blinked its welcome through the sleet and darkening sky. The attached diner was "The Pig Out Palace," and pig out we did. We stuffed ourselves for that day and hopefully the next, since the storm was closing the interstate exits.

Though mom and I did our best to overindulge at the diner, in God's economy, we are at our best when we keep our focus on the present. Each day is delivered with 24 hours for us to decide how we will make use of them. When we fill up on the worries of tomorrow or chew on the leftover troubles from yesterday, we spoil our appetite to take in the beauty of the present day that God has prepared for us. Only God knows our future, and He promises to give us exactly what we need. When we learn to entrust our yesterdays and our tomorrows into our Lord's care, we can start our day afresh to taste and see how good He is. After all, today is a gift—that is why it's called the present.

"A daily portion is really all we need. We do not need tomorrow's
supply, for that day has not yet dawned,
and its needs are still unborn.

Charles H. Spurgeon

MY PRAYER

"Dear Lord, sometimes I wander, and it is difficult for me to keep my focus on Your gift of today. Please help me to unlearn the habit of ruminating about the past and the future and learn the habit of keeping present in the joys of today. In Jesus' name, Amen."

WORSHIP

"One Day at a Time - Medley"
by Christine D'Clario, Josh Baldwin - Current

Not responsible for ads displayed on YouTube.

GIVING WINGS TO MY FAITH

What are some reminders you can incorporate into your daily routine to nudge yourself back into the present when your mind drifts into the worries of the yesterdays and tomorrows? One idea is to ask Jesus for His guidance for the day ahead before you put your feet to the floor—a surrender of your agenda to His.

I think we can all agree that Jesus knows best, so why not embrace the joy of a new day and ride upon the current of His love?

Philippians 4:19 • Matthew 6:34
Matthew 6:11 • Psalm 34:8

The P&O Meter

> "How beautiful on the mountains are the feet of those
> who bring good news, who proclaim peace,
> who bring good tidings, who proclaim salvation,
> who say to Zion, 'Your God reigns!'"
>
> Isaiah 52:7

We've all heard the saying, "Is your cup half full or half empty?" Basically, are you a "P" (pessimist) or an "O" (optimist)? I'm sure you have come across the folks in life who my mother refers to as Chicken Littles. Those who seem unable to go anywhere without hauling around their burden of worry. They tend to be generous in sharing their current sky-falling experiences, along with their dark clouds of doom. These are clearly the Ps. Then there are the Os.

These are the dear souls who carry sunshine in their hearts and are eager to share rays of encouragement, especially into cloudy souls. An ingredient of optimism is keeping a stash of laughter ready and handy for immediate use. The Proverbs tell us that a cheerful heart is good medicine. They also say that a happy heart makes a happy face. When we wake up each morning, we have a choice in how we will fill our cup. Let's make a pact to be those who choose to keep it half full and beyond!

QUOTE

"An optimist is the human personification of spring."
Susan J. Bissonette

MY PRAYER

"Dear Lord, there are times I struggle to keep a cheerful heart, especially when trying times surround me. Remind me to come to You to fill my cup with Your Presence, and to embrace Your joy so I may share Your light and sunshine with others. In Jesus' name, Amen."

WORSHIP

"Joy of the Lord"
by Rend Collective

Not responsible for ads displayed on YouTube.

GIVING WINGS TO MY FAITH

Put on some awareness goggles to double-check your P&O meter. If you find yourself struggling and sad, talk it through with Jesus and ask Him for His guidance on how to enter the realm of half full and beyond. He longs to fill you with His light, His life, and His joy—especially in challenging times.

Proverbs 17:22 • Proverbs 15:13
Romans 8:31 • Philippians 4:8,13

What Time Is It?

"There is a time for everything, and a season
for every activity under heaven."

Ecclesiastes 3:1

My little beagle, Ruby, suddenly shut down. She went to bed fine, then woke up incontinent and unable to walk. Her eyes at half-mast begged, "Help me." Stroking her soft little head, I whispered my question to Jesus, "What time is it?" As King Solomon so frankly scribed, there is a time for everything under heaven. A time to be born, a time to die. Was this the time for Ruby to leave this earth?

Here is an excerpt from Solomon's musing with some thoughts inserted in parentheses. A Time:

1. to Be Born (and born again)
2. to Die (to self)
3. to Plant (seeds of God's goodness)
4. to Uproot (weeds of selfishness)
5. to Heal (give and receive God's touch)
6. to Tear Down (walls between me and Jesus)
7. to Build (meaningful relationships)
8. to Weep (with those who weep)
9. to Laugh (open the windows of my soul to God's joy)

Only God knows the timing of every event under heaven—one of those secret things that belongs to Him. Seeing His hand at work through all of life's seasons provides a balm of peace, reminding us that we can trust Him. I am so grateful to share that, as of this writing, sweet Ruby is still in the land of the living. It just wasn't her time.

QUOTE

"My timing can lead to stress and striving,
but God says, 'Not so fast, my daughter.
Rest in My timing, My ways, and My rhythm."
Deborah Rutherford

MY PRAYER

"Oh Father, as the keeper of all time, only You know what lies ahead for me and my future. Help me to trust Your timing and to rest in Your rhythm. In Jesus' name, Amen."

WORSHIP

"Seasons"
by Benjamin William Hastings, Hillsong Worship

Not responsible for ads displayed on YouTube.

GIVING WINGS TO MY FAITH

1. Continue reading more of the passage in Ecclesiastes and add your thoughts to Solomon's.

2. Make it a habit to check in with the Timekeeper before charting your life's plans. Since Jesus knows all that lies ahead for you, trust Him to guide you and your decisions— even the small ones.

3. If you're in a season of waiting, take heart. God manages to run an on-time schedule. Read the verses below and tuck them into your heart as you trust Him in the wait.

Ecclesiastes 3:1-8 • Psalm 40:1-5
Isaiah 25:1 • Deuteronomy 29:29

Does Your Golden Need Some Polish?

> "So in everything, do to others what you would have them do to
> you, for this sums up the Law and the Prophets."
>
> Matthew 7:12

A few years ago, I was on an escalator in a shopping mall when my sandal somehow got wedged, and the metal grooves sliced deep into my pinkie toe. It began to bleed—badly. Grabbing tissues out of my purse did little to help. Once at the top, a woman who had been behind me sat me down, ran to a restroom, and got paper towels. No one else bothered to help. That dear woman did for me what she would have wanted done for herself.

As women of faith, Jesus is counting on us to lead by example. Life is busy with agendas and appointments, so "doing unto others" may make us late and even be a bit messy. But oh, the joy of serving the way Jesus would if He were here on earth. He is counting on us to be an extension of Him. That is why we must be available to represent Him—be His arms, His hands, His smile, His "doers." Grab the polish and let's shine up that Golden Rule.

Remember—in secret is best.

QUOTE

"Life's most persistent and urgent question is,
'What are you doing for others?'"

Martin Luther King, Jr.

MY PRAYER

"Dear Lord, may I never be too busy to be an extension of You and Your love in action to those I encounter who are in need. Use me to do for others what I hope others would do for me. In Jesus' name, Amen."

WORSHIP

"Lifesong"
by Casting Crowns

Not responsible for ads displayed on YouTube.

GIVING WINGS TO MY FAITH

Think of places within your community where you can reach out to those who are in need—to "do unto others." Here are a few ideas:

1. Volunteer at your local Food Bank or Meals on Wheels.
2. Visit a senior center, hospital, or someone who is housebound.
3. Ask your church about ways you can help meet a need.
4. Train your dog as a therapy animal to visit hospitals or nursing homes.
5. Prepare a meal for a new mom, a friend who is ill, or just because.
6. Plant some flowers for an elderly neighbor who is unable to.
7. Bake some extra muffins or cookies—share them with your neighbors.

You get the idea. Put your talents to use to spread the tangible love of Jesus.

Matthew 25:34-40 • Isaiah 58:10-11 • Proverbs 19:17

Would You Like That Gift Wrapped?

"Let him who walks in the dark, who has no light, trust in the
name of the Lord and rely on his God."
Isaiah 50:10b

It was three days before Christmas, and I was out shopping. For a suit to wear to my husband's funeral. Though he had not yet "crossed over," his time on earth was fading. His cancer had divided and conquered. My man of 32 years was leaving—for good. At the checkout counter, the cheerful saleslady asked if I would like my purchase gift-wrapped. Staring at her without seeing her, I shook my head no. Clearly, this was not a gift. Or was it?

Isn't it curious how such heart-wrenching events can make us stronger? It is now 11 years later, and when I look in the rear-view mirror at those days, months, and years clouded with sadness, I am reminded of how God managed to forge steel into the frame of who I am today. How grateful am I that He never leaves me alone in the dark but meets me in the halls of my pain. The box of darkness delivered onto my doorstep became a means for my Lord to display His glory. When I grasp His hand where His power is hidden, He leads me. "This is the way, Lisa. Hand in hand with Me."

That is the gift.

QUOTE

"Someone I loved once gave me a box full of darkness. It took me years to understand that this, too, was a gift."

Mary Oliver

MY PRAYER

"Oh Lord, as I reflect on my journey's draped in darkness that You have guided me through, my heart sheds tears of gratitude. How can I ever repay You for Your faithful care and kindness over me? You in me are my strength—my most wondrous gift. In Jesus' name, Amen."

WORSHIP

"I Look to You"
by Selah

Not responsible for ads displayed on YouTube.

GIVING WINGS TO MY FAITH

We have all encountered chapters of darkness in our lives. Take time with Jesus to journal about those times—what you have endured and where you are now. Express your gratitude for His care over you. Should there be lingering shadows, call on Jesus to illuminate them with His light and hang onto His hand tightly. His power is hidden there to empower you.

John 8:12 • Psalm 18:28 • Psalm 112:4 • Habakkuk 3:4

God's Mannequin

"Therefore, as God's chosen people, holy and dearly loved,
clothe yourself with compassion, kindness, humility,
gentleness and patience."
Colossians 3:12

I enjoy browsing online sites that lay out an entire outfit of clothing, offering mix-and-match possibilities to create different ensembles. Some feature women seamlessly changing from one look to the next, offering dressy or casual options, and then they whisk in the shoes and accessories to complete a put-together look. I thought of those clothing collections when I read the above verse.

What if, every morning when I dress, I intentionally "put on" God's attributes with each piece of clothing? A blouse of kindness, some jeans of humility, wrap a scarf of patience around my neck, and some sneakers of gentleness to get me on my way. As I step out, may I be God's mannequin displaying an example of Christ's nature to "shoppers" I meet throughout my day—those searching for the perfect fit of what He alone can fulfill. When Christ in me is beautifully displayed, it will stop a "shopper" in their tracks. They will want to know where to find what I have. And here's the perk— it's a free gift from God to all. No credit card required!

"Wear kindness and humility often. They are always fashionable."
Unknown

MY PRAYER

"Dear Lord, I ask that Your Spirit remind me as I ready myself for the day to not only dress nicely for what lies ahead, but to adorn myself with Your virtues that I might shine Your love and compassion to fellow life travelers who need Your touch. In Jesus' name, Amen."

WORSHIP

"Clothe Me in Your Grace"
by Risen Tunes (This is an AI-created song)

Not responsible for ads displayed on YouTube.

GIVING WINGS TO MY FAITH

Compassion—Kindness—Humility
Gentleness—Patience

These are "soft" qualities, and it takes practice to overcome the hardness of this life for these to shine through. Put some of your past days and weeks on replay to see how you have displayed Jesus in you.

Keep these five "softies" on a Post-it in your closet or on your make-up mirror as a reminder to wear them. Then step out, allowing the world to see you as God's beautiful mannequin.

Romans 13:14 • Proverbs 31:25
Colossians 3:12-17 • Isaiah 61:10

The Rise of Weeds

"Above all else, guard your heart.
For everything you do, flows from it."
Proverbs 4:23

I looked out my study window yesterday and saw that a weed had managed to grow larger than the shrub next to it in record time. It amazes me how weeds can grow so quickly and be so stinking healthy. I nurture my garden plantings with good soil and nutrients, encouraging their growth, then suddenly weeds sprout onto the scene, threatening a takeover.

The same can be said for the garden of our hearts. If we become complacent about what we allow to infiltrate our minds, we risk becoming infested with weeds of sin that can grow with a vengeance, choking out the goodness of God. Sin, as defined by the Bible, has become an accepted norm in today's culture. Since sin and God's righteousness cannot coexist, we must choose what we will plant, water, and nurture in our hearts. Just as in a dirt garden, weeds must be pulled out by their roots—the sins that can so easily entangle us. Lying, arrogance, lust, greed, and doubt are just the starter pack. Planting and tending a crop of thankfulness, love, mercy, patience, humility, and honesty not only allows less room for weeds but also creates a haven of beauty for others to glimpse the beauty of our Master Gardener. To behold the fragrant blooms of Jesus.

QUOTE

"Your mind is a garden, your thoughts are the seeds.
The harvest will bring either flowers or weeds."

Jackie Trottmann

MY PRAYER

"Dear Lord, please help me to keep my mind and heart aligned with Your Spirit so I can recognize the sins that long to entangle and trip up my relationship with You. Teach me to do the right thing and to tend to the garden of my heart diligently. In Jesus' name, Amen."

WORSHIP

"Guard Your Heart"
by 1GN

Not responsible for ads displayed on YouTube.

GIVING WINGS TO MY FAITH

1. The best way to recognize the sins that have become so widely accepted is to know and understand God's words of truth. Take inventory of any small or large thing that might prick your conscience and talk with Jesus about a remedy.

2. Be a Psalm 119:11 kind of girl—"I have hidden your word in my heart that I might not sin against you." Ask Jesus to reveal His ways and character, which He longs to cultivate in your heart. When you discover a nugget of God's truth from the Bible, tuck it in and memorize it.

Romans 12:2 • Colossians 3:5-10 • Hebrews 12:1
Ephesians 6:11• Matthew 5:6

The Q.T. Equation

"In quietness and trust is your strength."
Isaiah 30:15b

My now husband and I broke ground on what would become Fernwood, our sanctuary and home, beautifully situated in a cathedral of trees. But our want-to-be sanctuary began to face sky-high obstacles. COVID-19 invaded, crippling nearly everything; our contractor walked away from our unfinished home; the materials needed for building became scarce and even unattainable; and our wedding invitations had been sent for our upcoming wedding—at Fernwood. When my hair began falling out in chunks, I knew it was my wake-up call to slow down and settle myself. Isaiah provides our remedy for strength in The Q.T. Equation:

Quietness + Trust = Strength.

When chaos presses in, I must choose the voice of God over the noise of the problem. To not waste the precious time I have been given on this earth, to stress over matters I cannot control. To set aside time to rest in God's tranquility and settle into a confident trust with my Lord. To soak in His Presence like a warm bath. For it is in this sacred space that He will infuse me with strength, enabling me to hang the "No Vacancy" sign to anxiety, stress, and ultimately hair loss. I'm happy to report that we were married under an arbor in our woodland with a "mostly" finished home.

QUOTE

"I will never have this version of me again.
Let me slow down and be with her."

Rupi Kaur

MY PRAYER

"Thank You, my Lord, for allowing me to settle my racing thoughts and anxious heart in Your Presence. I long for Your strength to rise up within me to defeat the poisonous arrows of worry, fear, and anxiety poised to flood my mind and drown my tranquility. In Jesus' name, Amen."

WORSHIP

"In Quietness & Trust" by Julie True
Note: Though this song is a little longer, it is a "soaking" worship song. Allow it to usher you into the secret place of the Most High.

GIVING WINGS TO MY FAITH

1. If you haven't already, start journaling. Allow your pencil or pen the freedom to express onto paper what is preventing you from experiencing God's peace.

2. Dig deep and ask yourself, "Who am I trusting when I find myself in a 'situation'?" If it is anyone other than Jesus, make a plan to remedy that.

3. Find and memorize God's words to boost your trust in Him. Here are a few starters:

Psalm 143:8 • Jeremiah 17:7,8 • Isaiah 26:3,4
Proverbs 3:5,6 • Exodus 14:14

Fine Tune

"Do not let any part of your body become an instrument
of evil to serve sin. Instead, give yourselves completely to God,
for you were dead, but now you have new life. So use your whole
body as an instrument to do what is right for the glory of God."
Romans 6:13 NLT

We have a symphonic band here in our city, composed entirely of volunteers. My mother loves attending their concerts with friends from her senior living home and asked me to join them for the band's Christmas Concert. I was expecting a so-so performance with the old folks. Well, I couldn't have been more wrong. With a collection of 90 professionally accomplished musicians and guest vocal soloists, this orchestra was truly amazing!

Just as a conductor has musicians fine-tune their instruments before a performance, our Heavenly Father longs to meet with us before our daily performances. Each day offers a once-in-a-lifetime opportunity to play out the music of heaven—what it looks like to love Jesus so others can hear His sweet melody. Without tuning and practice, instruments can squawk and even grate on people's nerves. They can also fail to blend with the harmony of the orchestra. As our Father's instruments, we are gifted with our own unique tune in His vast symphony. It is up to us to learn the music and follow our Conductor's lead. When we do, I'll bet the angels give us a standing ovation!

QUOTE

“Your talent is God’s gift to you.
What you do with it is your gift back to God.”
Leo Buscaglia

MY PRAYER

“Dear Lord, use me as Your instrument, so that my talents and gifts may play the tune of Your kingdom and bring a smile to those around me. And may the bonus be, a smile on Your face as well. In Jesus’ name, Amen.”

WORSHIP

“Instrument”
by Matt Maher

Not responsible for ads displayed on YouTube.

GIVING WINGS TO MY FAITH

Take some time to identify the gifts and strengths that God has so meticulously woven into the fabric of your life when He created you. We operate so much better when we tune in to being and becoming all that God intended us to be. Offer yourself up for fine-tuning before heading into your day—your Conductor and His angels await your melody.

Psalm 150:1-6 • Romans 12:1 • 1 Peter 4:10,11

God's Recycling Bin

"And we know that in all things God works for the good of those who love him, who have been called according to his purpose."

Romans 8:28

Many years ago, when living in Los Angeles, the Waste Management folks delivered a small plastic recycling bin for newspapers. A novel idea to see if people would actually take to the concept. Well, fast forward, and we all know the answer to that. Recycling is now a common practice in everyday life, not to mention a worldwide topic.

And here's a newsflash. Our God just happens to be in the recycling business. Only He can take our mess-ups and recreate them into something good. Even our sins and mistakes can be recycled from trash into beauty through God's transforming power. I like to picture a bin at the feet of Jesus where I can place my poor judgment calls, my sins, my worries, and anything else that stains or burdens my soul. I have found that God's grace goes to work in that bin so long as I leave it there. Nothing is beyond the reach of God's vast storehouse of mercy. He's the God of do-overs and second chances—our ever-faithful recycling King.

"Dear Past, thank you for your lessons.
Dear Future, I am ready.
Dear God, thank you for giving me another chance."

Unknown

MY PRAYER

"Dear Lord, I humbly come before You, laying my baggage of sin and mess-ups at Your feet. Only You and Your grace can bring goodness from badness. Please forgive me and infuse me with Your power to overcome. In Jesus' name, Amen."

WORSHIP

"Grace"
by Michael W. Smith

Not responsible for ads displayed on YouTube.

GIVING WINGS TO MY FAITH

Develop a habit of regularly checking in with Jesus and asking Him to shed His light in your heart and your life. If you feel a nudge, surrender to whatever He reveals to you and place it in the bin. Be it worry, a bad mistake, a cave to sin, or careless behavior, ask for Jesus' forgiveness, accept it, and make a plan to keep that "thing" in the bin. Then watch and see the blooms of God's grace blossom in your heart.

1 John 1:9 • Isaiah 30:18 • Hebrews 4:16 • John 8:1-11

How to Hug a Porcupine

"Be kind & compassionate to one another, forgiving each other,
just as in Christ God forgave you."

Ephesians 4:32

I recently had an encounter with someone I have a close relationship with. Well, they managed to gob-smack me with rudeness and meanness, not just once, but on multiple occasions. Their quills got me. And boy, did it hurt.

We all have porcupines in our lives—those we're tethered to through work, family, neighborhood, and other ties, who can be unpredictable when they raise their quills to attack mode. After my painful punctures, I asked Jesus how to best handle porcupines. Here are some thoughts:

1. Keep your interactions to small doses.
2. Pray. Speak blessings over them, even under your breath, when engaged.
3. Keep your own quills down! Resist retaliation.
4. Kill it—with kindness.
5. Protect yourself and know your boundaries. Graciously exit the scene if necessary.
6. Forgive.
7. Refuse to allow the porcupine to puncture and drain life out of you. Keep fueled with promises of God's unfailing love for you.
8. If punctured, ask Jesus to heal you. The poison of bitterness sours you, not them.
9. Repeat #6 as often as necessary.

QUOTE

"Forgiveness doesn't excuse their behavior.
Forgiveness prevents their behavior from destroying your heart."
Unknown

MY PRAYER

"Dear Lord, I ask that you protect me and keep my heart safe and soft. Please teach me the art of forgiveness so that I might extend to others what You have so graciously given to me. In Jesus' name, Amen."

WORSHIP

"Forgiveness"
by Matthew West

Not responsible for ads displayed on YouTube.

GIVING WINGS TO MY FAITH

1. God can manage to use porcupines in our lives. Take some time with Him and ask, "What can I learn from my porcupine?"

2. Understand that this is not intended for an abusive situation. If abuse is involved, please seek out help. God never wants His girls in harm's way.

Luke 6:35 • Romans 12:14
Proverbs 11:16a • Matthew 5:44

Am I Interruptible?

"I solemnly appeal to you to proclaim the message.
Be ready to do this whether or not the time is convenient."
2 Timothy 4:1b-2a ISV

My husband recently took me by train for a weekend in Washington, D.C. While walking to Dupont Circle, I heard him behind me, "March, march, march!" I slowed my pace and laughed. My boys, when younger, said the exact same thing when I'd get in my "march" mode. I can easily tune out what is around me to accomplish my agenda.

The question then begs, am I interruptible? Or am I so focused on getting my world tamed to my liking that I miss an opportunity of availability to be ready for whatever Jesus might have on His agenda for me? His plan is the one I need to dial into my day, surrendering my To-Do list for Him to rearrange if necessary. When I remind myself that I am not the general manager of the universe and allow Jesus to be my navigator, I can tune into the day He has planned for us to do together. And when an untimely interruption arises, I can respond with a heart of grace rather than an "I'm too busy marching" attitude. If Jesus had time for interruptions, so should I.

QUOTE

"An inconvenience is only an adventure wrongly considered.
An adventure is an inconvenience rightly considered."

G.K. Chesterton

MY PRAYER

"Dear Lord, please remind me to commit my agenda to Your master plan. My heart's desire is to walk in tandem with you, and to slow my march to the tempo of your Holy Spirit. In Jesus' name, Amen."

WORSHIP

"Available"
by Elevation Worship

Not responsible for ads displayed on YouTube.

GIVING WINGS TO MY FAITH

1. Take some moments of quiet reflection to think of where and when you have been taking the role of a general and asking God to "fall in."

2. Choose a brief prayer or a Bible verse that speaks peace to your soul. Write it down on a small card and keep it close— tucked in your pocket or propped on your desk—as a gentle invitation to surrender to Jesus throughout your day. When we surround ourselves with His truth, letting go becomes a holy habit.

Job 22:21,22 • John 3:30 • Luke 10:25-37

Those Plan Bs

Three summers ago, my granddaughter arrived for our annual "Camp Gia." I am Gia, Grandma in Action, and I had to live up to my title after arriving at our adventure for the day—the big pool. Upon finding they had closed early, baby girl was devastated. To plug her tears, I told her we had Plan B, which I was concocting on the fly. We bombed off to the market, grabbed a cart, and headed to the freezer aisle, where I instructed her to pile in all the ice cream she wanted. Once home, we turned on the garden hose and had our first Hose War, eating gobs of ice cream in between. That Hose War is one of Charlie's best memories, and we now hit the repeat button every summer.

Though far more momentous than a closed pool, I cannot help but draw the parallel to those chapters of life that manage to crash and burn, leaving my hopes in piles of smoldering ash. Crestfallen dreams ending in death—be it emotional, relational, or physical—are my cue to dial into the God of Plan Bs. The one who collects my heap of embers, transforms them into beauty, then gently takes my hand and leads me to the intersection of Hope and a Future.

QUOTE

"Draped in darkness alone and spent,
My heart seeks You and Your content.
Rise up, awake, my spirit strong!
To blend my soul with Thy belong."

Lisa W

MY PRAYER

"How grateful I am for You, my Lord, that in my darkest hours, I can place my hand into Your hand and trust the plans You have for me. Only You can take my shattered dreams and transform them with Your beauty. For this, I am ever grateful. In Jesus' name, Amen."

WORSHIP

"When I Don't Know What to Do"
by Tommy Walker

Not responsible for ads displayed on YouTube.

GIVING WINGS TO MY FAITH

1. Take a moment to think about the losses you have survived and thank God for His guidance over you during those times. Remembering our altars of faith helps to build our trust for the here and now.

2. Is there someone you know who is experiencing loss? Reach out with a heart of God's love and hope to encourage their hurting heart.

3. Be prepared! Life is all about Plan Bs. Know God's promises. They help to navigate you through the boulevards of Difficulty and Pain.

Proverbs 16:9 • Proverbs 19:21
Isaiah 55:8,9 • Genesis 50:19,20

The Ruffled Mind

"In peace I will lie down and sleep, for you alone, O Lord,
make me dwell in safety."

Psalm 4:8

Last night, my mind was swirling with a carousel of thoughts. A looming family crisis was begging for my mind's permission to be swept into the land of worry and fret. One of those o'dark thirty wake-up calls barging into my sleep, intent on robbing my peace and arresting my rest. I invited Jesus into my thoughts to not only stop the anxiety train but, more importantly, ask for His Presence to intervene miraculously. I recited Psalm 23 more times than I could count, though my sleep continued to elude me.

Morning has now come, and over coffee and my journal, I am choosing to reflect on the great goodness of God in my life. God does not need this reminder; I do. I call to mind His wondrous provision in guiding me through valleys, deserts, and numerous "impossibilities" where Jesus stepped in and made a way where there was no way. Because of my Lord's great love for me, I am not consumed. His compassions never fail. How great is His faithfulness! In You, my Lord, my soul finds its rest.

"A ruffled mind makes a restless pillow."
Charlotte Bronte

MY PRAYER

"Oh Lord, I surrender my ruffled thoughts into Your care. I trust You and know that all things will work together for good. I hold tightly onto this promise for me and my family—for today and always. In Jesus' name, Amen."

WORSHIP

"Rest"
by TobyMac, Terrian, Gabe Real

Not responsible for ads displayed on YouTube.

GIVING WINGS TO MY FAITH

Since those middle-of-the-night wake-up calls can be random robbers of our sleep, consider in advance how to handle the invasion. As this may look different for each of us, ask Jesus for guidance on the best approach for you. Some ideas: call to mind God's verses of promise beginning with each letter of the alphabet; pop in some earbuds, and listen to scripture, soothing music, or even get up and down. Up out of bed and down onto your knees to lay it out before our Lord. Make a note of the "situation" in your journal or Bible margin, including the date, so you can circle back to see how Jesus shows up for you. My notes are documented ... stay tuned!

Philippians 4:6,7 • Matthew 11:28
Proverbs 3:24 • Psalm 16:7-9

The Winning Trio

"With what shall I come before the Lord and bow down
before the exalted God? He has showed you, O man, what is good.
And what does the Lord require of you? To act justly, and to love
mercy, and to walk humbly with your God."

Micah 6:6a & 8

I remember waking up one morning and asking Jesus, "How can I put a smile on Your face today?" I wanted more than anything to honor my Lord for His ongoing kindness toward me. When I came across this verse in Micah, God's answer was illuminated across the pages in my Bible—"To act justly, love mercy, and walk humbly with Me."

I set aside dedicated time to have a think on this trio that God required of me. Putting pen to paper, I went to work to figure out how to implement these into my life and my world. As God's children, we are uniquely designed with varying strengths and talents. And here is a little cherry on the whipped cream—when we live out the life that God has specifically woven into us, we thrive. How wonderful it is to ignite our passions and God-given talents to act justly, love mercy, and walk humbly with our Lord. May the Lord smile on you and be gracious to you as you navigate this day ahead, incorporating this winning trio.

QUOTE

"Those who walk with God always reach their destination."
Henry Ford

MY PRAYER

"Dear Lord, may my heart learn to speak and sing the language of heaven so that I might honor You through my actions, my love of mercy, and walking humbly with You. In Jesus' name I pray, Amen."

WORSHIP

"Act Justly, Love Mercy, Walk Humbly"
by Pat Barrett

Not responsible for ads displayed on YouTube.

GIVING WINGS TO MY FAITH

Make an appointment with yourself to take some time to ponder these verses, and especially this trio that God requires of us. Jot down your thoughts as you ask Jesus how to best incorporate these into your day-to-day life. When we act, love, and walk with Jesus, we no doubt put a smile on His face.

Matthew 9:13 • James 2:13
Luke 6:32-36 • Numbers 6:25 NLT

The Infusion & the Spillage

"Thy kingdom come, Thy will be done in earth, as it is in heaven."
Matthew 6:10 KJV

I have a friend who is a beloved pastor here in town who has taught me, along with our community, the significance of The Lord's Prayer. After all, Jesus Himself told His disciples, "This, then, is how you should pray." When Pastor Pete prays this prayer at the top of his services, he adds the name of our city after "thy will be done in earth *and in our city*, as it is in heaven." This has inspired me to include my own additions for God's will to be done in the here and now, as it is in heaven.

I was thinking this week about God's kingdom coming in me and through me, and what that might look like. I visualized the effects of dry ice. You may remember those punch bowls at Halloween parties with a chunk of dry ice in them. The vapor from the ice wafts over the sides, spilling onto and down the table. This is how I pictured God's kingdom in me. As God's container, His kingdom is tucked inside my heart. When I ask His Spirit to flow over me, it ignites my heart, and I cannot help but to spill over with the essence of God—His love, His grace, His kindness, and yes, His beauty. And the bonus? Unlike dry ice, God's Presence never melts!

QUOTE

"The seeking of the kingdom of God is
the chief business of the Christian life."
Jonathan Edwards

MY PRAYER

"My Father, who is in heaven, holy is your name. May your kingdom come here and now in my life that I might be filled with Your Presence and let it spill over and onto others that they too can experience Your love. In Jesus' name, Amen."

WORSHIP

"The Lord's Prayer"
by Il Divo

Not responsible for ads displayed on YouTube.

GIVING WINGS TO MY FAITH

1. Pray through The Lord's Prayer, pausing on each phrase to reflect on its meaning in your life. If Jesus tells us to pray this way, we should do it—fresh from our hearts, not just a memorized script in our heads.

2. Ask the Holy Spirit to ignite your heart so you are empowered to share the gift of God's kingdom and make a difference to those God has arranged appointments for you to meet.

Matthew 6:5-13 • 1 Corinthians 6:19
Matthew 6:33 • 1 Peter 3:15

The Ultimate Rip

"My God, my God, why have you forsaken me?"
Matthew 27:46b

Early in my career, I worked with a woman who lost her pre-teen daughter to cancer. In her words, "it ripped her heart out of her chest" to have to bury her sweet girl. I ran into her years later, only to find that her heart had never recovered from her loss. She had been irreparably damaged.

There was a Father who also suffered an immense loss—God the Father. For God chose not to send a messenger or an angel, but rather, He allowed the Trinity to rip itself apart, sending Jesus as the sacrifice for all mankind's sins. That fateful day unveiled a galactic triumph, a cosmic victory of the ultimate sacrifice. The day the Spirit groaned in unbearable agony and the Father turned His back, for He could not bear to witness the crush of evil and sin heaped upon His Son. The day the angels wept. That sacred and scandalous day of Jesus' crucifixion—securing our bridge to eternity. When death fell on its face at the foot of the cross, where it remains to this day. Jesus, the priceless gift at an unimaginable cost.

From tragedy to triumph.

<h1 style="text-align:center">QUOTE</h1>

The collide of the cross and my sin with its stain,
ripped open the veil where His holiness had lain.
God freed His pure Presence from an ark of gold gild,
He now invites me, my clay jar, to be filled.
The ultimate and most costly invitation.

Lisa W

MY PRAYER

"Oh, Lord, may I never underestimate the gravity of Your immense sacrifice for me. My soul and my spirit bow in reverence, humbly accepting Your invitation for life with You, and without end. Help me make my heart Your eternal home. In Jesus' name, Amen."

WORSHIP

"Beautiful Scandalous Night"
by Sixpence None the Richer, Bebo Norman

Not responsible for ads displayed on YouTube.

GIVING WINGS TO MY FAITH

1. Spend some quiet time alone, just you and Jesus, to contemplate God's great sacrifice. His death unto life gift for you. Keep a journal nearby to allow your thoughts to flow with gratitude for what this gift means to you.

2. Be a willing heart to give to others what has been generously given to you. Ask Jesus at the top of each day who He might have in mind for you to share His gift of life with. Counteract the flood of ominous news reports with the "Good News" of life with Jesus.

Matthew 27:1-54

What Will You Choose?

"'Martha, Martha,' the Lord answered, 'you are worried and upset
about many things, but only one thing is needed. Mary has chosen
what is better, and it will not be taken away from her.'"
Luke 10:41,42

Some of us with a few more candles on our birthday cake might
remember a daytime show from the 1970s, *The Dating Game*. It
featured a bachelorette asking questions to three bachelors who were
hidden from her view. After hearing their answers, the girl would
choose her date. Sometimes, you could see the "oh no!" look on the
bachelorette's face at the reveal if she had whiffed on her choice. It
seemed like a dreamy idea to be whisked off on a fun and
adventuresome date, but it all hinged on the guy whom the girl chose.

Research shows that we make about 35,000 decisions every day.
That's a lot of choosing! The range varies from subconscious
choices to life-changing decisions. God has intricately wired our
brains to manage all of this, although He knows we need some
behind-the-scenes help to keep it running smoothly. When we
surrender our will and bow to the power of Christ in us, a holy
moment unfolds when Jesus whispers, "You have chosen what is
better." I, for one, do not want to be the girl who whiffs and makes
"oh no!" choices. This life is far more precious than just a bad date.

QUOTE

“She realized she had this one. This big, bold, and beautiful life. And she realized she didn’t want to live it chasing and crying and apologizing. Starving and fearing and regretting. She realized she wanted to live it proudly and freely and creatively. Lovingly and fully and sweetly. She realized she could choose. And so, she chose.

Cara Alwill Leyba

MY PRAYER

“Dear Lord, I want to declare here and now that all of me chooses all of You. I bow in surrender and ask that You have Your way in my life. In Jesus’ name, Amen.”

WORSHIP
“I Choose Jesus”
by Moriah Peters

Not responsible for ads displayed on YouTube.

GIVING WINGS TO MY FAITH

Set aside some quiet moments to contemplate God’s amazing gift of “free will.” You’re not a pre-programmed robot but a unique woman beautifully created to contain and carry the Presence of Almighty God. Reflect on the significance of this gift and how your daily decisions, even small ones, impact you and those around you. If Jesus nudges you to make some adjustments, talk it through with Him and align your choices to His true north. Never underestimate the power of your ability to choose. Make a choice to choose well.

Deuteronomy 30:19,20 • Joshua 24:15
1 Chronicles 28:9 • Revelation 3:20 • Psalm 1:1-3

Without the Smell of Smoke

> "They saw that the fire had not harmed their bodies, nor was a hair
> of their heads singed; their robes were not scorched, and there
> *was no smell of fire on them.*"
>
> Daniel 3:27b

My now husband and I decided to get married under an arbor in the woodland behind the home we had built together. So that is exactly what we did. Afterwards, we celebrated with family and close friends, serving up a shrimp boil and beautifully laden tables of charcuterie. We ended the evening beneath the stars and string lights, making s'mores around our fire pit. The next day, when we all gathered for brunch, we noticed how the smell of the fire had managed to cling to us from the night before.

The three young men we read about in Daniel refused Nebuchadnezzar's edict to exchange their worship of God for worship of a golden image. So, it was that they were thrown into a blazing furnace—so intense, it killed the soldiers who threw them in. But once inside, they had a visitor. Jesus joined them and chatted with His devoted sons, keeping them completely cool and refreshed. Unlike our bonfire, the young men exited the furnace without the smell of smoke and, beyond that, unsinged and unharmed. When the heat gets cranked up, you can count on our God of consuming fire to not only be with you but to rescue you and leave you without a trace of the smell of smoke.

QUOTE

"It's not about God putting out your fires.
It's about Who is in the fire with you."

Unknown

MY PRAYER

"Dear Lord, how grateful I am for Your care over me. Even in times of great distress and pain, You are with me and keep me safe and secure—even in the fire. Though 'thank you' seems inadequate, please accept my offering of gratitude to You. In Jesus' name, Amen."

WORSHIP

"Another in the Fire"
by Hillsong UNITED

Not responsible for ads displayed on YouTube.

GIVING WINGS TO MY FAITH

We all face "in the fire" chapters at various times in our lives. Reflect on your fiery times and give yourself a review. How difficult was it to keep from complaining and falling victim to self-pity? Are there lessons from those fires that you can think of to put to use during any future furnace experiences? Read the account in Daniel 3 to give your faith a boost and never forget you are not alone—even in the fire.

Isaiah 43:2,3 • Psalm 66:12 • Zechariah 2:5

The Alien Affect

"But our citizenship is in heaven. And we eagerly await a Savior
from there, the Lord Jesus Christ, who, by the power that enables
him to bring everything under his control, will transform our
lowly bodies so that they will be like his glorious body."
Philippians 3:20-21

My late husband was British and moved to the States soon after we met. We eventually married, and he became a Resident Alien. We went on to have two sons who found it quite amusing when their father would bellow in his illustrious British accent, "I am an ALIEN!" while chasing them through the house.

In the same way, as heirs of Christ, we are aliens. Our spiritual passports do not come from this earth but from the Celestial City, where God reigns in His kingdom and eagerly awaits our arrival. No matter that our origin of birth is *here*, our destiny is being meticulously prepared *there*. When we become new creatures in Christ, our earthly citizenship is exchanged for a new one that reads, "Permanent Residency in the Kingdom of Heaven." So, we must be diligent to conform to our new culture, learning its language and adapting to its customs.

Friending people of a like heritage aids in accustoming us to our destined eternal home, along with studying our User Manual, the Bible. *"The free gift of God is eternal life in Christ Jesus our Lord."* Spread the word—God has sent His invitation, and the gates of this glorious Kingdom are wide open for all to enter.

QUOTE

"If I find in myself desires which nothing in this world can satisfy, the only logical explanation is that I was made for another world."

C.S. Lewis

MY PRAYER

"Dear Lord, I am an open vessel longing to learn Your culture and speak Your language. Help me to be and become all that You have created me to be, spreading Your out-of-this-world love and Your invitation of life to others. In Jesus' name, Amen."

WORSHIP

"Because He Lives"
by Celtic Worship

Not responsible for ads displayed on YouTube.

GIVING WINGS TO MY FAITH

1. How are you preparing for your arrival in the Celestial City? Life on this earth is but a fleeting moment. Consider what you might do to break loose from the customs of this life and conform to the cultures of Christ.

2. What does it mean to be transformed by the renewing of your mind?

Romans 12:2 • John 18:36a
2 Corinthians 5:17 • 1 Peter 2:9-11

Fill'er Up

"Let the morning bring me word of your unfailing love,
for I have put my trust in you."
Psalm 143:8a

I am a To-Do list kind of person. I keep my lists front and center to help me remember all my awaiting tasks. It's a struggle for me not to get swept up in my to-dos when I start my day. When making my coffee, tasks beckon—the flower vases need fresh water, the dishwasher needs emptying, and the morning sun rays highlight the dog hair on the floors that need a Swiffer. Before you know it, to-dos have trumped my morning, and worse yet, they have stolen my time to Fill'er Up.

In my younger years, there were service station attendants who would gas our cars. "Fill'er up with ethyl!" was the request for my Pontiac Firebird. Just as we need to refuel (or nowadays charge) our cars, our Heavenly Father longs to meet us to fill our empty tanks, preparing us for what lies ahead. Since we have no idea what our day might bring, we must trust that Jesus knows our journey and all we will need to get through it. Mornings with Jesus should be at the top of our list for tuning our engines to ready our ride for the day. It is even highly recommended in our User Manual, the Bible. So why not Fill'er Up?

QUOTE

“Good morning, This is God.
I will be handling all your problems today.
I will not need your help,
so sit back, relax, and have a great day!”

Unknown

MY PRAYER

“Dear Lord, please remind me to take the time to refuel in Your Presence, for I cannot be of service to You and to others when my tank is on empty. Thank You for Your grace and care over me. In Jesus’ name, Amen.”

WORSHIP

“Good Morning”
by Mandisa ft. TobyMac

Not responsible for ads displayed on YouTube.

GIVING WINGS TO MY FAITH

If you would like to make a date with Jesus in the mornings, create the space. Have a chair or sofa where you are comfy; prepare a coffee or tea in a special mug or glass; light a candle, put on an instrumental worship playlist, and make certain you have your tools handy—your Bible, devotional, and journal. Make it an occasion. After all, you are meeting with the King!

Isaiah 50:4 • Psalm 143:8 • Psalm 90:14 & 17 • Psalm 5:3

What's in a Name?

"She will give birth to a son, and you are to give him the name
Jesus, because he will save his people from their sins."
Matthew 1:21

When my number two son and his wife were expecting their first
child, I received a call. "How am I supposed to do this, Mama, not
even knowing who this child is?" The gravity of choosing a name
for his soon-to-be son or daughter weighed heavily on my son. In
the end, his baby girl received the same name that would have been
given if they had a son—Charlie in honor of my late husband,
Geoffrey Charles. Personally, I was just grateful they didn't call
her Geoffrey!

When the angel Gabriel visited Mary, he delivered an unbelievable
spoiler alert—she would soon become pregnant with a son, and no
need to fuss over a name. You are to name him Jesus, the name
above all other names. And by the way, your baby will become king,
for a kingdom that will never end. Mercy! Can you even imagine
that visit and that download? Jesus—what incredible power to be
bundled up in such a tiny infant—the Savior of the whole world,
the Son of the Most High, the ruler of God's kingdom. At this
name, Jesus, EVERY knee will bow, and EVERY tongue will
confess that Jesus Christ is Lord!

QUOTE

"Take the name of Jesus with you everywhere you go; breathe it
everywhere in prayer. Be loyal; be holy; Live for God,
and God will confirm His word."

William Marrion Branham

MY PRAYER

*"My dear Jesus, how I love Your name. I am so grateful that You are my
Savior and that You know my name. I surrender my heart to You and
long to follow You all of my days. In Your beautiful name, Amen."*

WORSHIP

"What a Beautiful Name / Agnus Dei / WT Session"
by Travis Cottrell feat. Lily Cotrell

Not responsible for ads displayed on YouTube.

GIVING WINGS TO MY FAITH

Spend some quiet moments alone with your journal. Reflect on
the name of Jesus and how He impacts your life. This will look
different for each of us, so there are no right or wrong answers.
Simply take note of what Jesus means to you. Before ending your
time with your Savior, don't forget to say, "thank you."

Luke 1:26-38 • Philippians 2:9-11 • Acts 4:12 • Isaiah 9:6

Drop Your Anchor

"We have this hope as an anchor for the soul, firm and secure."
Hebrews 6:19a

Sitting in the front row of one of Los Angeles's oldest and most beautiful churches, I listened to the hymn, "It Is Well With My Soul," with my eyes closed. When I opened them, I was staring at my husband's casket. I chose this hymn for his service as a reminder for me and, hopefully, for others as well. Although waves of sadness and grief were desperate to engulf my soul, I prayed this song in that moment as my anthem to Jesus, prompting my aching heart to embrace the very words that Horatio Spafford tucked into his heart when he penned this song after tragic loss came his way.

Tragedy—not if but when—will strike us all. Though my husband had fallen to the sword of cancer, I had not. Navigating the weeks and months ahead was clouded with a myriad of challenges. Grief behaves differently for everyone, and there is no pat answer to what and what not to do. Except for one. To keep the compass of your heart firmly oriented to your True North, so when storms arise, your soul is securely anchored to Jesus and His promises. It is a holy hope we hang onto so we too can lift our voice and sing, "It is well, it is well with my soul!"

QUOTE

"When peace like a river attendeth my way,
when sorrows like sea billows roll;
whatever my lot, Thou has taught me to say,
"It is well, it is well with my soul."

Horatio G. Spafford—1873

MY PRAYER

"Oh Lord, how I thank You that my hope in You is not wishful thinking. It is grounded trust, anchoring me to Your throne, where I am securely moored to You. In the peace-filled name of Jesus, I pray, Amen."

WORSHIP

"It Is Well"
by Kristine DiMarco

Not responsible for ads displayed on YouTube.

GIVING WINGS TO MY FAITH

Sit quietly with Jesus to reflect on who or what you are anchored to. Is your dependence on your spouse or a family member? Is it clinging to an addiction or a bad habit? Are you feeling secure in yourself or your occupation? Take a thoughtful inventory and talk it over with Jesus. Be open to pulling up the anchor that can fail and dropping anchor with Jesus. The only firm and secure option for our souls.

Isaiah 26:3,4 • Isaiah 33:2
Psalm 33:20-22 • Psalm 34:18

Life in the Stoop

"You give me Your shield of victory, and your right hand sustains me;
You stoop down to make me great."
Psalm 18:35

When my boys were young lads, we lived within walking distance of a corner store filled with candy displays that this Mama deemed off-limits. When my late husband would come home from work, the boys would squeal over each other, begging to be hoisted onto their Papa's shoulders for a ride to the forbidden treats. From their father's shoulders, they viewed their world from a different perspective.

I think of that scene when I read the above verse. God never leaves me in the trenches, but rather, He stoops down, swoops me onto His shoulders, and carries me to victory despite the battle raging below. Not only does my Savior sustain me, HE MAKES ME GREAT! Whatever may come my way, I have a God who desires to see me not only succeed, but to do so with greatness. We would do well to take note of our Lord's unfailing compassion over us and be mindful to pass it on to others. To never be too busy to aid a fellow life traveler in need of a boost.

P.S. I'll bet you East Coasters thought this was about the front entrance steps to your home. I'll have to write a devotional for those kinds of stoops on another day!

QUOTE

"There is a loftier ambition than merely to stand high in the world. It is to stoop down and lift mankind a little higher."

Henry Van Dyke

MY PRAYER

"My dear Lord, what would I do in this life without You and your consuming passion over me? I can hardly fathom that You, the God of the universe, would take notice and raise me up to make me great in Your kingdom. From my most grateful heart, Amen."

WORSHIP

"You Raise Me Up"
by Selah

Not responsible for ads displayed on YouTube.

GIVING WINGS TO MY FAITH

1. If you are in the trenches and need a "lift," today is a good day to do just that. Take some moments with Jesus and ask Him for His stoop and swoop—a fresh perspective from atop His shoulders.

2. Be on the lookout for ways you can be the arms of Jesus to help someone who may need a "lift." Trust me, the blessing will be all yours!

Psalm 3:3 • Isaiah 41:10
Deuteronomy 33:12 • Isaiah 40:31

Scars—How Will They Tell Your Story?

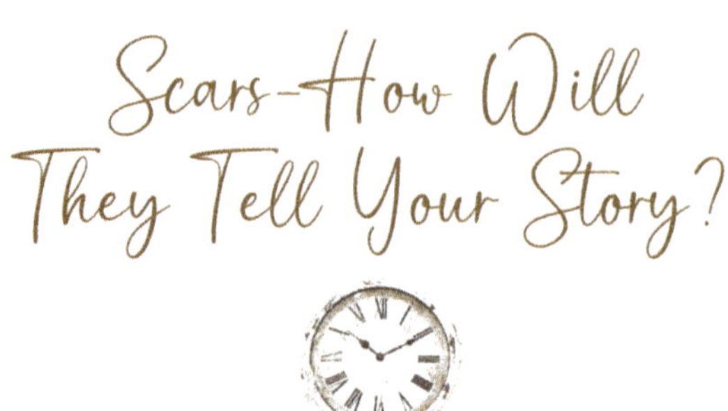

"But he was pierced for our transgressions, he was crushed for our iniquities ... and by his wounds we are healed."

Isaiah 53:5

Scars. We all have them. Not the ones that plastic surgery can fix, but inner scars that are left behind from painful wounds. A fractured relationship, the loss of someone dear, a betrayal, a bad mistake we have made, and so on.

Here's a thought: could it be that the scar you now carry is a reminder of what God has brought you through? Instead of fixating on memories of the pain, shift your focus to the grace that God has afforded you. Your scars tell a story that says, "I survived." In this broken life, we *will* face troubles and pain. Jesus even says so. Then He encourages us to take heart! He has overcome. Jesus, our Good Shepherd, longs to carry us through the pain and into His wings of healing. Wear your scars as badges of victory, showing others what it looks like when we cling to our overcoming God of hope. Those healed-over wounds that have left the scarring are now your story— your overcoming, your victory. Surrender your scars to Jesus. He gets it. He, too, has scars. You can trust Him in the pain as you allow His scars to heal your scars.

QUOTE

"Scars remind us of where we've been.
They don't have to dictate where we are going."
David Rossi

MY PRAYER

"Dear Lord, thank You for bearing the unbearable for me and overcoming evil and death. Your willingness to be scarred unto death to rescue me from this life and its brokenness overwhelms me. Help me hold tightly onto Your nail-pierced hand. In Your name, Amen."

WORSHIP

"Scars in Heaven"
by Casting Crowns

Not responsible for ads displayed on YouTube.

GIVING WINGS TO MY FAITH

1. Do you have any healed-over wounds that still cause you pain? Sit quietly with Jesus and talk with Him about it and write your thoughts in your journal.

2. Try viewing your wounds as badges of victory, displaying the strength and grace God gave you to get you on the other side.

3. When you're ready, be open to sharing the story of your scars with others who need to know that there is hope and healing in Jesus.

John 16:33 • Jeremiah 30:17 • Luke 24:37-40
Psalm 147:3 • Romans 8:18

How Much Longer, O Lord?

As I was chatting with Jesus this morning about a situation I've been praying over for many years, memories of my two pregnancies came to mind. The anticipation, the waiting, and especially the little one I could not wait to meet. Each week marked a milestone in my baby's development, along with changes in my expanding body to accommodate the growing life inside me. As I flipped my calendar to the 39th week, my very pregnant body begged, "How much longer?" Impatience crept its way in and was trumping my excitement and anticipation.

Believing in God and His promises can produce that same feeling of frustration when we are "in the wait." Whether it's waiting for a healing, a breakthrough, or for God's love to capture the heart of a wayward loved one, we must surrender our timetable to the most perfect Timekeeper and trust the wait. God is always on time to deliver that pending miracle.

QUOTE

"I am not a woman with great faith.
I am a woman with a little faith in the great God!"
Kathryn Kuhlman

MY PRAYER

"Dear Lord, how I thank You that even during my moments of restlessness and doubt, You are with me and at work behind the scenes. Even when I can't see what is happening, I choose to trust You in the wait. In Jesus' name, Amen."

WORSHIP

"Believe For It"
by Cece Winans and Lauren Daigle

Not responsible for ads displayed on YouTube.

GIVING WINGS TO MY FAITH

Waiting is a lonely journey that we were never meant to endure alone. Surrounding ourselves with a sisterhood of faith-filled women provides life-giving infusions of hope for our weary, impatient hearts. Seek out that tribe in a church or Bible study to join forces with, not only as a receiver, but also as a giver. Something holy happens when we allow God to use our own places of pain to extend hope to a hurting heart.

Isaiah 40:29-31 • Psalm 13 • Mark 10:27

A Life of Passion

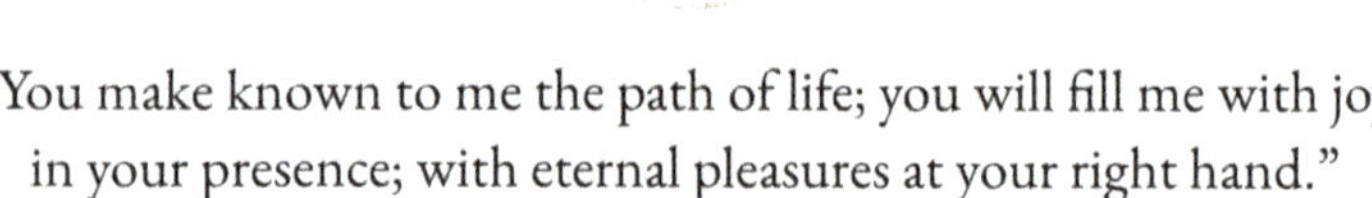

> "You make known to me the path of life; you will fill me with joy
> in your presence; with eternal pleasures at your right hand."
>
> Psalm 16:11

Quaintrelle (quaint-relle) (n) \'kwānt-'rel\– A woman who emphasizes a life of passion, expressed through personal style, leisurely pastimes, and cultivation of life's pleasures.

I read this definition and decided right then and there that becoming a Quaintrelle sounded right up my alley. The only problem was that my life had been trapped in years of deep sadness and overwhelming obstacles, making it seem unachievable for me. But Jesus always manages to somehow, some way untwist the turns and do what I call a "Clean up on Aisle 5." He not only mops up the mess, but He manages to beautify it.

I am here to say that, though it took many years, Jesus allowed the Quaintrelle in me to make a debut. So much so that I once told a girlfriend that I felt like I was living in a magazine article! True story. Only Jesus can take brokenness and create wholeness, unveil pleasures that satisfy the desires of my heart, and turn a girl with a downtrodden soul into a Quaintrelle proclaiming the goodness of God in the Land of the Living. My true passion is Jesus, who has been so faithful and so kind to me, His blossoming Quaintrelle. Who knew! Well, Jesus surely did.

QUOTE

"My mission in life is not merely to survive,
but to thrive; and to do so with some passion,
some compassion, some humor, and some style."

Maya Angelou

MY PRAYER

"Father, I surrender the desires of my heart into Your care. You have designed and created me with longings and aspirations to enjoy in this life. I trust you to ignite my passions in Your perfect time. From your most grateful Quaintrelle, Amen."

WORSHIP

"I Give You My Heart"
by Hillsong Worship

Not responsible for ads displayed on YouTube.

GIVING WINGS TO MY FAITH

Take some time to think of one passion or leisurely pastime that has been put on the back burner due to unforeseen obstacles, busyness, or simple neglect. Jot down an achievable step you can take this week to begin to cultivate this passion. Each week, take a few more steps toward making this a reality. Don't forget to commit it to Jesus, thanking Him for the "pleasures forevermore" He has tucked into His right hand—just for you.

Psalm 20:4,5 • Psalm 37:4 • Psalm 27:13

96

If Your Knuckles Are White, Let Go

"... All the days ordained for me were written in your book
before one of them came to be."

Psalm 139:16b

Many years ago, I was training to get my pilot's license. The day came when my instructor asked me to pull the plane to the side of the taxiway, and he got out. It was time for me to take my first solo flight. Before shutting the door, he said, "Don't worry, Lisa. God is your co-pilot!"

I loved that idea and began chatting with Jesus as if He were sitting right next to me while flying in the skies above Los Angeles. Then, just the other day, I came across this: "If God is your co-pilot, you may want to switch seats."

But of course! I'd always thought of God as my co-pilot, which I considered a good thing, but now I see it differently. Even though I may be piloting a plane, Jesus must always remain the Pilot of my life. Only He knows the flight plan He has meticulously charted for me and can safely navigate me through it. As I calibrate my compass to my True North and surrender my seat of control to Jesus, He guides me through this journey called life.

QUOTE

"If God is your co-pilot, you may want to switch seats."

Unknown

MY PRAYER

"Oh, Lord, I surrender my life to You and trust You as my Pilot as You unfold the plans You have charted for me. Please help me let go of things that are beyond my control and entrust my journey to You. In Jesus' name, Amen."

WORSHIP

"Jesus Take the Wheel"
by Carrie Underwood

Not responsible for ads displayed on YouTube.

GIVING WINGS TO MY FAITH

1. A good practice to embrace is to check in with your Pilot before lifting your head off your pillow each morning. A friend of mine says, "Lord, what shall we do today? You go first!" Then, fasten your seatbelt.

2. Take some quiet moments alone with Jesus to align your compass and ask Him to show you where you need to loosen the grip of control and surrender it to Him. Then, switch seats. I think we'd all agree it is a much safer way to travel through life.

Proverbs 3:5,6 • Job 11:13-19 • Matthew 11:28-30

Lay it Out There

"Hezekiah received the letter from the messengers and read it.
Then he went up to the temple of the Lord
and spread it out before the Lord."

2 Kings 19:14

I have two girlfriends who have been in my world for over 50 years. Growing out of pimples and into adulthood, we have maintained a strong bond throughout the years. Annual Girlfriends Getaways are a must, but even more sacred is the Fire Bell. It is activated only in an emergency, when we drop everything to be there for each other. In the safety of three, we divulge our "situation" and lay it out there.

King Hezekiah rang his Fire Bell when he received a letter from an enemy king who mocked God, vowing to destroy Israel. This evil king had a resume of victories to support his threat, sending Hezekiah straight to the temple to spread the blasphemous letter before God. He then proclaims how mighty He is, shifting his focus from the problem to the Problem Solver. God answers him by saying, "The zeal of the Lord Almighty will handle this." What happens next is nothing short of amazing as God's zeal springs into action. That night, an angel of the Lord wipes out 185,000 men in the enemy camp! Whatever situation you face, do as Hezekiah did and lay it out before the Lord and watch His zeal unfold.

"I have held many things in my hand and have lost them all. Whatever I have placed in God's hands, that I still possess.
Martin Luther

MY PRAYER

"Dear Lord, I humbly lay my troubles out before You and acclaim You as my Lord and King. I thank You that Your power is at work on my behalf. I surrender and lay out my issue before You on the wings of Your zeal. In Jesus' name, Amen."

WORSHIP

"Lay It All Down"
by United Pursuit feat. Will Reagan

Not responsible for ads displayed on YouTube.

GIVING WINGS TO MY FAITH

The next time you have a situation that threatens to interrupt your peace, try this: write it down and lay it out before the Lord. It can be at the altar of your church, on a dining room table, or kneeling at your bed. Just get it from your heart to God's ears. Put God squarely between you and your problem. Then read the passage below to remind your faith that God is mightier than any obstacle you will ever face!

2 Kings 18-20

God's Secret Service Agents

> "For He shall give His angels charge over you,
> to keep you in all your ways."
> Psalm 91:11 NKJV

I love skeet shooting, but my enthusiasm manages to surpass my skill, so my husband took me to a shooting range for a lesson. After hitting one of the more challenging clays, the instructor mentioned that our ex-Vice President had been there the day before and had struggled to hit that same target. When we asked about his security, we were told they were definitely there but kept themselves obscure.

Did you know that God has deployed Secret Service Agents to watch over you? In Psalm 23, we read that Goodness and Mercy follow us all the days of our lives and therefore, always have our backs. (Have you ever turned around to thank them?) In 2 Kings 6, the prophet Elisha saw the hills filled with horses and flaming chariots—the Heavenly Host Army outnumbering the enemy's army. God tells David in 2 Samuel 5 that when he hears the marching in the tops of the balsam trees, he is to move quickly because it signifies that the Lord and His heavenly host army have gone ahead to defeat the enemy. The next time you feel vulnerable or afraid, remind yourself that God has His agents at work on your behalf. Although they may be obscure and largely unseen, never underestimate God's protection and provision over you. You never know what may be poised to defend you in the treetops!

QUOTE

"Few people realize the profound part angelic forces
play in human events."

Billy Graham

MY PRAYER

*"O Lord, I pray You open my eyes and senses to the awareness of Your
angels and Your protection You provide. Let me never be remiss in
offering You my gratitude for taking such amazing care of me.
In Jesus' name, Amen."*

WORSHIP

"Whom Shall I Fear (God of Angel Armies)"
by Chris Tomlin

Not responsible for ads displayed on YouTube.

GIVING WINGS TO MY FAITH

Read the passages below, then close your eyes and visualize the
unseen realm—the angels of the Lord at work on your behalf. If
you are interested in learning more about angels, I'd like to
recommend an excellent book I've read by Billy Graham, *Angels:
God's Secret Agents.*

2 Samuel 5:22-25 • Psalm 23:6 • 2 Kings 6:15-17
2 Kings 19:34,35 • Psalm 34:7

It's Okay to Be Fresh it's Even Recommended

"Because of the Lord's great love we are not consumed, for His compassions never fail. They are new (fresh) every morning."
Lamentations 3:22,23a

Were you ever told as a child, "Don't get fresh with me!" Well, your Heavenly Father says the opposite. He loves fresh, and He delivers fresh every single morning. I must admit that I am a girl who enjoys a plethora of fresh—fresh coffee, fresh berries for breakfast, fresh sheets on the bed, fresh flowers on my kitchen island, the smell of fresh cut grass, to name just a few.

As I woke up this morning, our window was cracked open, and the birds were so happy that the sky had finally run out of rain. I took a deep breath of the fresh air filling our bedroom, and the above verse rippled through my thoughts. A fresh dose of God's mercy and kindness had awakened me to begin my day. I then thought about how I could return God's kindness. So, I offered up a dialogue of gratitude for His morning gifts and made a pact to throw out anything stale between Him and me. More than fresh coffee or sheets, I want my love for Jesus to be on refreshment mode every single day.

QUOTE

"Every day is a new window of God's mercy and grace!
Don't bring seeds of yesterday's struggles
into the fertile ground of today."

Bishop Gary Oliver

MY PRAYER

"Dear Lord, my heart longs to deepen my love for You. Please nudge me when things feel a bit stale on my end so I might freshen up my relationship with You. In Your merciful name I pray, Amen."

WORSHIP

"Your Unfailing Love – Psalm 143:8-10" by Sherri Youngward (feat. Taylre Nelson)

Not responsible for ads displayed on YouTube.

GIVING WINGS TO MY FAITH

Here are some ideas to revitalize your faith and keep it fresh in Jesus:

1. Make it a priority to spend time in devotion to Jesus— through prayer, meditating on a scripture of significance, or reading the Bible. Life is complicated, and God gets it. That's why He provided us with His User Manual, filled with His promises to help us through.

2. Find a way to "get lost" in God's love over you. Maybe through worship and song, strolling through nature, or gathering with other faith-filled life travelers.

3. Pass it on. Something within us ignites when we share the freshness of who and what Jesus means to us. Don't be shy. EVERYONE needs God's love. We were made for it.

Isaiah 50:4 • Psalm 86:15,16 • Psalm 143:8-10
Ephesians 2:4,5 • Psalm 19:7-11

What's in Your Fruit Bowl?

"But the fruit of the Spirit is love, joy, peace, patience, kindness,
goodness, faithfulness, gentleness, and self-control."
Galatians 5:22,23a

Over the years, I've kept a full and enticing fruit bowl on the kitchen counter. I'm not sure how successful it was in luring my boys to indulge in "healthy," but I tried. If I could get them interested in some of the "fun" fruit, I'd hoped to overtake their sugar radar with an option that wouldn't rot their teeth. I find the same to be true of the fruits of God's Spirit, beautifully laid out for our taking.

1. Love vs. Selfishness
2. Joy vs. Sadness of Heart
3. Peace vs. Anxiety
4. Patience vs. Frustraton
5. Kindness vs. Intolerance
6. Goodness vs. Evil
7. Faithfulness vs. Disloyalty
8. Gentleness vs. Harshness
9. Self-Control vs. Indulgence

The first nourishes our soul, while the latter rots us from the inside out. Choosing to embrace these virtues requires a willing heart and discipline. Although not one of us can attain perfection, with determination to conquer the enemy of our soul and plant these seeds of the Spirit, we cling to our Vine. Fill your fruit bowl with the bounty of the harvest and be ready to pass it around to others.

QUOTE

"You cannot plant seeds of sin and expect a crop of goodness.
Jesus says it best, 'You will know them by their fruit.'
There is nothing sweeter than being a fruit stand for Jesus."

Lisa W

MY PRAYER

"O Lord, I surrender myself to You, my Master Gardener, to till the soil of my heart. Please help me to protect and cultivate the seeds that you plant in me that I might be fruitful for You. In Jesus' name, Amen."

WORSHIP

"Selah III (Fruits of the Spirit)"
by Hillsong

Not responsible for ads displayed on YouTube.

GIVING WINGS TO MY FAITH

Take some time to inventory your "fruit" and the virtues you display in your journey through life. Pray for God's guidance and grace over the areas that are in need, making any necessary adjustments. Be on the lookout for any rot that gets between you and others, and more importantly, between you and Jesus.

Keep it sweet.

John 15:5,16 • Matthew 7:16,17
Ephesians 4:22-24 • Colossians 3:8-10

Flip the Switch

"The unfolding of your words gives light;
it gives understanding to the simple."
Psalm 119:130

My late husband and I were asleep in our home in Studio City when the 1994 Northridge Earthquake rocked our world in the middle of the night. The eeriest thing was how pitch-black everything became after the quake. As we sat in the supposed safe zone of our home, we could not even see our hands in front of our faces. Nor could we see our baby boys that we were holding. The switch had been flipped to "off" in the entire city of Los Angeles.

Living in darkness is not only disorienting in the physical world but also in the spiritual realm. Without the Light of the World shining His rays of truth into our hearts, we are left to wander in obscurity, stumbling our way through life. God's words illuminate our path, showing us the way we should go, especially when we hit a fork in the road. I have a girlfriend who has memorized the book of Philippians along with other passages of Scripture. Although I struggle to remember people's names, she assures me we all have the capacity to tuck chunks of God's words into our minds and hearts. If it means more of Jesus in me, then I'm definitely giving it a try.

QUOTE

“I cannot tell you how much I sometimes long for the Bible.
I read it daily, but I would really like to know it by heart
and to see life in the light of that phrase,
‘Your word is a light for my path and a lamp for my feet.”

Vincent van Gough, letter to Theo van Gough, 1877

MY PRAYER

*“O Lord of beauty and grace, thank You for rescuing me from darkness
and bathing me in Your glorious light. Help me to store Your words in
my heart so that I might shine brightly for You. In Jesus’ name, Amen.”*

WORSHIP

“Thy Word”
by Michael W. Smith and Amy Grant

Not responsible for ads displayed on YouTube.

GIVING WINGS TO MY FAITH

There have been times I’ve draped my open Bible over my head,
wishing God’s words could tumble from the pages and settle into
my mind. But since that is nonsensical, you might find other ways
to get those words memorized and tucked in. Some ideas include
prayer walks, note cards, singing songs of Scripture, inviting a friend
to join you, and, as my friend does, incorporating hand motions.
There’s also good old YouTube. Whatever method works for you,
find it and flip the switch!

John 8:12 • Psalm 119:11,105
Proverbs 6:20-23 • Ephesians 5:8

The Fury of Your Love

"The Lord thundered from heaven; the voice of the Most High
resounded. He shot his arrows and scattered the enemies, great
bolts of lightning, and routed them."
Psalm 18:13,14

Ten weeks after my son's first open-heart surgery, he started training
with his eighth-grade football team. Driving home after the third day
of practice, my rearview mirror reflected his face. It was wet with tears.
I gently pressed only to hear that his coach had called him a "zero
factor" during practice—in front of the entire team. The hairs on my
neck stood to attention. Did this guy not realize that we kept sick bags
in the car for my boy to throw up in after each practice because his
lungs had been compromised from being on the heart-lung machine
for so long? That the physical exertion he gave to the sport he loved
made him physically ill? Well, the following day, the coach was
introduced to my fury. He had crossed the line with me.

Though my fury is no match for God's, that is exactly how our Lord
feels about us, His beloved. The earth trembles. He exhales smoke and
fire. He parts the heavens, mounts the cherubim to soar on the wings
of the wind to rescue you. All because He delights in YOU. How can
we but love such a God as this?

P.S. My tenacious boy went on to land a 30-minute Thanksgiving
spotlight on Fox Sports—a testament to his athleticism and
courageous comeback. Never a zero. Always our hero.

QUOTE

"You, my Lord, are waves of relentless passion pouring over me.
In surrender of heart, I hold fast to the fury of Your great love."

Lisa W

MY PRAYER

*"My dear Lord, my heart surges with deep gratitude and awe for
Your passion over me. I long to serve you all my days as my worship
unto you. In Jesus' name, Amen."*

WORSHIP

"How Can I But Love You"
by Tommy Walker

Not responsible for ads displayed on YouTube.

GIVING WINGS TO MY FAITH

Read through Psalm 18:4-19 several times. Sit and visualize the rich
imagery that the Psalmist, David, is portraying in this song, which
he sang after the Lord delivered him from his enemies and the hand
of Saul. If you are in a "situation," call on your God of Psalm 18 and
let this King of Hearts win your heart.

Psalm 18:1-19 • Zechariah 9:14-17
Deuteronomy 33:26,27

Snowflakes & Kindness

"Whoever pursues righteousness and kindness will find
life, righteousness, and honor."
Proverbs 21:21 ESV

It snowed this morning. I watched the small flakes flutter from the sky, marveling in wonder at their individuality. So gentle, so pure, and oh so beautiful. The flakes amassed themselves as they landed, creating a smooth frosting of pristine white. Kindness and snow must be kin. They quietly arrive, leaving in their wake an array of beauty. To glisten in the sunlight and shimmer in the moonlight, these flakes gently cover blemishes without judgment.

This life is full of challenges and difficulties. When we make the effort to sprinkle God's kindness onto withered souls weary in their journey, something beautiful transpires. Jesus is introduced and displayed. By paying forward the kindness that He has lavished onto us, the Proverbs tell us we receive a bonus pack of life, righteousness, and honor. What am I waiting for? I must get busy finding ways to impart the kindness of Jesus into parched souls in need of a fresh snowfall of God's love.

QUOTE

"Life is short.
And we do not have much time
to gladden the hearts of those
who travel our way with us.
So, be swift to love, make haste to be kind.
And go in peace to love and serve the Lord."
From a journal entry, December 16, 1868
by Henri Frederic Amie

MY PRAYER

"Oh Lord, may I make haste this day to spread Your kindness to a fellow life traveler. Use me as Your vessel to share Your sparkle and to cheer a weary heart with Your great love. In Jesus' name, Amen."

WORSHIP
"Kindness"
by Steven Curtis Chapman

Not responsible for ads displayed on YouTube.

GIVING WINGS TO MY FAITH
Be intentional with kindness. Chat with Jesus right now about who might need a note, a visit, a mere smile, or ____________________. (You fill in that blank.)

Beware: This may cost you money and/or time. But that cost pales in the overflow of blessings that will return to you.

P.S. As best you can, let this be a "you and God" thing. Read Matthew 6:1-4 to find out why.

Ephesians 4:32 • Hebrews 13:1,2 • I Peter 3:8,9

What's Your Issue?

"Jesus turned and saw her. 'Take heart, daughter,' he said, 'your faith has healed you.' And the woman was healed from that moment."

Matthew 9:22a

In my final moments before becoming a missus, my father wrapped his arm around mine and held on tightly to my trembling hand. Kissing my cheek, he then walked me down that garden aisle to give me to my soon-to-be husband. That walk with my father is in the 'much-cherished' section on my shelf of memories.

There is one woman whom scripture records as sharing her own father-daughter moment with Jesus. This woman was in a desperate situation. She was impoverished, ceremonially unclean, extremely ill, and suffering. Her issue? Twelve years of hemorrhaging. Her desperation drives her to her last resort—Jesus. Remnants of her dwindling hope ignite themselves as she pushes her way through the crowd. "If only one touch, and I will be healed." Reaching for His cloak, her fingers sweep His hem. Then comes a surge of power. She feels it, and so does Jesus. At once, she knows she is healed. Jesus stops and turns to find her, then locks His eyes with hers. Knowing she needed Him so badly, he tells her, "Daughter, your faith has made you well." Nowhere else in Jesus' recorded words is this tender address of "daughter" found. A cherished Father-daughter moment that changes everything in this woman's world. Though we are never told her name, we do know her faith was the runway to heal her issue instantly.

QUOTE

"Oh, trembling heart, the cries of your pain
have pierced the ears of God Himself."

Unknown

MY PRAYER

"Oh Father, as your daughter, I reach out for You as I humbly lay my issues at Your feet. Ignite my spirit with sparks of faith so that I might receive Your power to meet me in my pain and heal my wounds. I am ever grateful for your love and care for me. In Jesus' name, Amen."

WORSHIP

"One Touch"
by Nicole C. Mullen

Not responsible for ads displayed on YouTube.

GIVING WINGS TO MY FAITH

In your quiet and private moments with Jesus, talk with Him about whatever "issues" you might be facing. Is there a bleed in your life that is leaving you weak and drained? If so, take heart. Ask Jesus to step into the issue and stop the bleed. There is nothing too embarrassing or too complex for Jesus to heal. It only takes one touch.

Mark 5:25-34 • Isaiah 41:13
Ephesians 3:20,21

The Forecast for Today Is ...

"When you pass through the waters, I will be with you; and when you pass through the rivers, they will not sweep over you."

Isaiah 43:2a

My weather app is my go-to whenever I plan to head out or host a gathering with grilling, cornhole, and s'mores around the fire pit. Once armed with the info, I plan accordingly. If we have a funky weather forecast and I'm entertaining, I'll activate Plan B on our wrap-around porch. If venturing out, I'll slip into my hound dog rain boots, don my yellow raincoat, and grab an umbrella.

Life as we know it is like the weather—unpredictable and often catches us unprepared. Jesus Himself told us in John 16:33 that we'll face storms. "In this world, you *will* have trouble (pressure, affliction, or tribulation). But take heart! I have overcome the world." I love this verse—especially the exclamation point. Did you hear that? Jesus has overcome everything for you. No matter what blows into your life, take heart! You have Jesus to navigate you through the storm. When you open your spiritual weather app, the Bible, you prepare and strengthen yourself for "bad weather" that comes your way. So, instead of feeling overcome, lean into the Overcomer. Bottom line, the forecast for today is all clear with Jesus by our side.

"The storm will not destroy you.
It will prove the strength of your Anchor."
Unknown

MY PRAYER

"Dear Lord, I confess that I can become overwhelmed with worry and anxiety when life presents unexpected and troubling turns. Please help me lean into You, my eternal Overcomer and steadfast Anchor. In Jesus' name, Amen."

WORSHIP

"Praise You in the Storm"
by Casting Crowns

Not responsible for ads displayed on YouTube.

GIVING WINGS TO MY FAITH

Take some time to create a spiritual emergency preparedness plan for storms. Just as you keep flashlights, candles, and even food rations for emergencies, plan what you can do to be ready for spiritual storms. Because it's not a question of *if*, but *when*. As God's girls, let's heed the Girl Scouts' motto and "Be Prepared."

Mark 4:35-41 • Isaiah 30:21 • John 14:27 • Ephesians 6:10-17

The Beauty Blender

"You are altogether beautiful, my love; there is no flaw in you."
Song of Solomon 4:7 ESV

My four-year-old granddaughter was watching me put on my makeup one morning when she piped up and asked, "Hey Gia, where's your beauty blender?" I was a bit surprised she even knew what a beauty blender was, so I held up my foundation-smeared fingers. She just shook her baby girl head at me. Her mama was once a makeup artist and no doubt had shown my sweet girl the correct way to apply makeup, which I clearly did not adhere to.

That beauty blender moment got me thinking about how God sees us. One touch from Him and He creates us with incredible care, weaving purpose and unique talent into our beings. No matter how broken, how shameful, or how far we have wandered from His Presence, God sees us as He made us. A creation He marvels over—a masterpiece He treasures. God covers every imperfection with His beauty and grace and sees no flaw in us. The day will come when we will live in full expression of the awe and wonder that God has meticulously crafted into each of us. Until then, put your face to the Son to allow His beauty to radiate into you and through you.

QUOTE

"The other day I looked in the mirror, and I didn't feel very pretty.
So, I said, 'God, I need a reminder. What do you see
when you look at me?' So, He said, 'You are my beloved,
my perfect creation. Beautiful.' So, I said, 'Yeah, but what do
others see when they look at me?' So, He said, 'They see Me.'
And suddenly I felt beautiful.

Maddiehodgett.wordpress.com

MY PRAYER

"Dear Lord, please help me see myself as You see me—Your masterpiece—fearfully and wonderfully made. And remind me to see others the same way—as Your masterpiece—fearfully and wonderfully made. In Jesus' name, Amen."

WORSHIP

"The Truth"
by Megan Woods

Not responsible for ads displayed on YouTube.

GIVING WINGS TO MY FAITH

1. Have an honest conversation with yourself, asking, "What qualities do I possess and exhibit that I might allow God to touch and enhance with His beauty blender?" Journal your thoughts and notes to keep as an encouragement and reminder.

2. Surrender all of you into the care of your creator, Jesus. Explore your passions and talents that lie dormant. Discover how to ignite those God-given gifts He so purposefully wove into you. There is only one "you." Let your light shine!

Psalm 139

FTMGGOTP

"... and overflowing with thankfulness."
Colossians 2:7b

I am utterly useless at understanding messages that use acronyms or initialisms. I get BBQ, FYI, and of course, LOL. But toss in IMO, IRL, ICYMI, and even G2g, and I'm at a loss. There is one initialism that I use often, which is mine and mine alone: FTMGGOTP. I bet it would even stump ChatGPT. That's because it's a personal thing between me and Jesus. I found myself beginning to use this, spelled out in full, when journaling. It was after my first husband had made his journey Home to Jesus. I had volumes of emotion pouring from my heart, landing onto the pages of my journal. The journal that endured my falling tears, broken pencil leads, and then managed to keep itself in shape when flung across the room.

Over time, my heart was able to empty itself of its grief, pain, rants, and anger, eventually making the turn into gratitude as I purposed to view life through the lens of thankfulness. I had survived. Jesus never abandoned me, and along the way, I built my altars of faith as God's promises leapt from my Bible and personified themselves in my life. It was then that this sign-off to Jesus emerged:

From The Most Grateful Girl On The Planet

"And she survived the hard days, with God leading her through.
His way was perfect. His way was blessed.
And no step would she ever take alone."

Lauren Fortenberry

MY PRAYER

"My dear Lord, how priceless is Your loving care over me. You take me by the hand and guide me through valleys looming with shadows and death, and lead me beside your still waters of rest. How can I ever repay you for Your kindness to me? With love, From The Most Grateful Girl On The Planet, Amen."

WORSHIP

"Adore"
by Jaci Velasquez

Not responsible for ads displayed on YouTube.

GIVING WINGS TO MY FAITH

If you find yourself in a valley, circle back to your altars of faith where Jesus has come to your rescue. Don't be shy. Express your gratitude to Him for His faithfulness in past situations, then thank Him for all He promises to do to take care of you going forward. And get it onto paper—if you think your journal can handle it!

Psalm 23 • Psalm 100 • Psalm 107:31,32 • Psalm 138:1-3

I would be remiss if I did not provide you with a "How To" plan of:

HOW TO DO LIFE WITH JESUS

A Guide to Experiencing Deeper Faith in God:

1. First, you must choose to want to take this journey with God. Simply let Him know you desire to blend your life with His. Since this is what you were created for, this is as natural as taking a breath. A simple surrender of your heart into God's hands: "Lord, I want to do life together with you. Please show me and teach me how to do this. I thank you, Jesus, for forgiving me of my shortcomings and sins and for securing eternal life for me when You died on the cross. Help me to be and become the person You created me to be and to love you with my whole heart."

2. Now that you have established a friendship and relationship with God, take time to talk with Him. This is commonly known as prayer. Chat with Him throughout the day about whatever is concerning you or on your mind. Whatever concerns you, concerns God. He is ALL about you and loves you with unbridled passion.

3. Take time to learn about your God. Get a Bible and begin in the book of John, the Psalms, and the Proverbs. It is also

helpful to get a devotional to help you focus and navigate through God's User Manual.

4. Begin to memorize nuggets of Truth from God's love letters to you. Your Bible is your treasure box filled with promises from God's heart to yours. When you tuck His truth into your mind and heart, your faith will begin to bloom. There are lists of God's promises online that you can print out.

5. Find your tribe and your place to belong. Dialing into a place of worship is important. This looks different for everyone. Seek out a church that you feel comfortable in with people who share your interests. Make sure they pass this test in their belief department:

   - The Bible is the God-breathed words of life

   - Salvation is by grace through faith

   - The Trinity—The Father, His Son, Jesus, and the Holy Spirit.

Then dive in and get involved in doing life with folks on the same team!

6. Worship is your spirit communing with God's spirit. Crank up some music that exalts God and get lost in your thoughts of loving Jesus. Whatever flavor of music that speaks your language is the one for you.

7. Share your God adventure with others, allowing the love poured into you to overflow. You never know the difference it may make in another person's life when you freely spill the love of Jesus.

May God bless you as you journey into a deeper faith and love of Jesus!

And My Gratitude Goes to ...

First and foremost, it is You, my Jesus. Without You and Your constant Presence in my life, I have no idea where I would be. Certainly not here. That is why I cannot help but brag on You.

FTMGGOTP
(See Devotion #60 for translation)

David, my man, my husband, and my rock. My love, you bring me such joy and happiness—who knew! Well, to be honest, Jesus did. And bless you for not thinking me a kook, especially when I refuse to check my Bible in my airline baggage. And by the way, I forgive you for taking our dogs' affection hostage with your endless supply of "cookies." You win.

To the tribe of women in my life who, along with my mother, cheered me to the finish line, my soul is steeped in thankfulness. You all know who you are. And especially you, Victoria, you saw what I couldn't see and put the order in to "just do it!" I thank you, and even that pitchfork!

Katrina Moody, whose expertise and unwavering support were the compass that navigated me through the edit-to-publish journey. You took what felt like a tangled-up ball of yarn and helped weave it into a beautiful throw, ready to warm the hearts and souls of our readers—all while managing your own challenges. My heart bows in gratitude to you.

Pastor Pete, what a gracious gift you are to us all. Without you, I wouldn't have had a platform. However, I have a confession: you'll note I "borrowed" your "Putting Feet to My Faith" with just a slight alteration. Sorry, but it's a good one!

My beloved WFF Farmington and Glenmore Girls, you have been so generous in your support of me. As I struggled with jitters and stutters during my 'training wheels' phase, you embraced me and encouraged me to grow into my voice and my speaking. My heart beats happy for the gift of each one of you.

And lastly, I thank you, my dear Reader, for making the time to *Take Ten to Turn Up*. It is my prayer that these devotions will gently guide you into the beautiful and sacred dance of life with Jesus.

Credits

Cover & Interior Design by Katrina Moody and Lisa W
Book Formatting by Katrina Moody
Illustrations by Lisa W
Photo by Emily White
Inspiration by the Holy Spirit

Soli Deo Gloria

Meet Lisa W

Lisa W is a woman-to-women storyteller who loves Jesus. It is her joy to weave chapters of her life experiences to showcase a God of hope. Her fresh and unique presentations encourage women's hearts as she unveils God's truths and His unwavering promises.

Lisa retired after 45 years in the film and television industry. She laughs when she says that she finds promoting Jesus far more rewarding than Hollywood entertainment. "Well, isn't that a no-brainer?"

She and her husband live on the East Coast in a home she describes as their sanctuary, beautifully situated in a cathedral of trees. It is there that their two hound dogs occasionally allow them use of the sofa.

Stay tuned for the release of:

- *My Journey in Joy & Gratitude – A One-Year Journal*
- *Take Ten to Turn Up:*
    Volume № 02 Devotional – Hint of Cypress Edition
- *P R O V I S I O N S – Recipes & Such*

All three are at work in her typewriter, awaiting their debuts. Visit www.lisawtalks.com for updates along with Lisa's "Take Ten Chats," her ten-minute talks of inspiration.

If you would like to invite Lisa to speak at an upcoming event, retreat, or conference, visit her website at www.lisawtalks.com/catch-me-live and send her a request. She would love to hear from you.

"Some people like PB & Js.
I happen to thrive on JB & J.
Jesus, Bible, & Journal"

A Little Gift for You

The Worship Playlist

Ready to create a sacred space in a busy world?
Scan the QR Code below to visit my website
www.lisawtalks.com#theworshipplaylist
where you can "Dial In" to access
the 60-song worship collection from

Take Ten to Turn Up – Volume № 01 Devotional

It is the prayer of my heart that these
melodies provide a gentle lift for your
spirit and a steady anchor of hope for your soul.
May you feel God's goodness in every note.
Be blessed as you worship!